Objective Questions in Marketing

Objective Questions in Marketing

B.R. Sangale
G.Y. Shitole • R.M. Sable

ADHYAYAN
ADHYAYAN PUBLISHERS & DISTRIBUTORS
NEW DELHI (INDIA)

Published by
ADHYAYAN PUBLISHERS & DISTRIBUTORS
4378/4B, 105, J.M.D. House, Murari Lal Street
Ansari Road Darya Ganj, New Delhi - 110002
Ph.: 011-23263018, 011-23277156, Fax: 23280028
Email: adhyayanpublishers@yahoo.com

Objective Questions in Marketing

Edition 2011
ISBN 978-81-8435-247-4

Printed in India

Published by Harish Chandra Yadav for Adhyayan Publishers & Distributors, Delhi. Laser Typesetting at Jain Computers and Printed at Tarun Offset Printers, Delhi

PREFACE

Marketing is a core and specialized area of study in commerce and management. The universal functions of marketing are buying, selling, transporting, storing, standardization and grading, financing, risk taking &market information. How these functions are performed by different marketers globally has made marketing a dynamic subject & its study has been a challenge to students. Substantial increase in global trade has further extended the scope of the subject. E-commerce has given rise to a central marketplace which is located in the cyberspace. Thus students need rigorous training to familiarize with the dynamics in the subject and the style of competitive exams.

It is against this background that the authors have undertaken the task of bringing out an all objective question format book in contemporary areas of marketing for competitive exams. The book covers ten vital areas of study in marketing. Each chapter has questions ranging from concepts to various techniques and their evaluation. The questions are organized in a sequential and logical way to get a holistic view of the subject. A deeper understanding of the principles will help in building confidence in students.

A special feature of the book is the inclusion of a chapter on international marketing keeping in mind the increasing role of marketing in a global economy. Another notable feature of the book is the practical and application oriented questions based on numerous brands and corporate strategies. Such question solving exercise will help in strengthening the understanding of the subject and enables readers to stretch their thoughts to actual happenings in the market.

The book is an initiative to help students to crack competitive examinations organized by State Service Commissions, Union Public Service commissions, various nationalized banks, insurance companies etc. The students of commerce and management shall be benefited with the objective type questions given in the book.

The authors have taken utmost care to make this the best resource book for aspirants. We welcome constructive criticisms from students and feedback for improvements, changes and developments for subsequent editions.

Editors

Contents

1

GENERAL MARKETING

1. The increase in the worth of a product as a result of activities it passes through distribution chain_______.

a] value added by marketing

b] augmented product

c] user oriented marketing

d] integrated marketing

2. The theory that believes that retail innovators are the pioneers of growth cycle of marketing _______.

a] weakest link theory

b] retail promotion theory

c] wheel of retailing theory

d] combined target market approach

3. The theory that states that certain parts of a product wear out first is _______.

a] weakest link theory

b] value analysis

c] depreciation theory

d] none of the above

4. A firm fully controlled and owned by a parent company_______.

a] secondary co.

b] unit co.

c] holding co.

d] wholly owned subsidiary

5. **The system when prices of market leader's item are frequently changed ______.**
   a] vertical pricing
   b] variable leader pricing
   c] strategic pricing
   d] periodic pricing

6. **A method of segmentation based on the rate at which consumers buy products is ______.**
   a] usage rate segmentation
   b] consumption based segmentation
   c] benefit segmentation
   d] valve segmentation

7. **________ is a system in which each product is assigned a ten digit pre-marked number in the form of bar code.**
   a] Universal product code
   b] Product computer code
   c] National product code
   d] Market product code

8. **________is a promise made in a highly competitive manner which positions the product clearly in the minds of consumer.**
   a] USP
   b] POP
   c] Value addition
   d] Product appeal

9. **________ is a strategy in which large firms maintains prices of products at a level higher than necessary to protect smaller competitions from furious competition**
   a] Strategic pricing
   b] Differentiated pricing
   c] Umbrella pricing
   d] Premium pricing

10. __________ is a strategy where no attempt is made to address to individual market segment

a] Specific segmentation

b] Demographic segmentation

c] Undifferentiated segmentation

d] Psychological segmentation

11. A method of forecasting sales for existing products is _______.

a] projection

b] estimate

c] trend extension

d] market forecast

12. The geographical zone containing the people who are likely to purchase firms goods or service

a] consumer cross-section

b] trading area

c] market

d] commercial centre

13. The value added to a product when it is available at the proper time the customer wants is _______.

a] value addition

b] time utility

c] specific utility

d] customized product

14. Short term business planning when focussed on implementation of organizations long term strategic goal.

a] periodical planning

b] target oriented planning

c] tactical planning

d] strategic planning

15. A place where people exchange goods for which they no longer have a need is called _______.

a] gray market

b] swap market

c] black market

d] social marketing

16. Superette is a _______.

a] grocery super market

b] general store

c] departmental store

d] small retail outlet

17. Developmental cost that are unrecoverable are _______.

a] Sunk cost

b] Shut down cost

c] Capital cost

d] Non-recurring cost

18. To establish proof of a claim is _______.

a] validity

b] substantiation

c] evidence

d] trust

19. When the buyer requires a product without modification it is a cose of _______.

a] repeat purchase

b] recorder

c] straight rebuy

d] approved demand

20. A strategy in which prices are maintained at the level charged in the mature stage of PLC is ______.

a] administered pricing

b] rich aversion pricing

c] status quo pricing

d] maturity pricing

21. __________ is a store which carries a single product category & sells at below regular retail prices.

a] Speciality store

b] Shopping centre

c] Premium goods store

d] Speciality discount store

22. The social forces influences which affect the operation of market place is ______.

a] market forces

b] societal forces factor

c] economic forces

d] environmental factors

23. The individual needs which are concerned with basic protection & physical well being are ______.

a] Ego needs

b] Esteem needs

c] Safety needs

d] Prestige needs

24. A pricing strategy aimed at elimination of uncertainty in the marketing environment is called ______.

a] risk aversion pricing

b] specialized pricing

c] segmentation pricing

d] status quo pricing

25. A trade practice in which markets attempt to control the price at which the products will be sold at subsequent steps of distribution is called ______.

a] administered pricing

b] status quo pricing

c] resale price maintenance

d] psychological pricing

26. A strategy aimed at reviving demand for a product is called ______.

a] remerchandising

b] remarketing

c] repositioning

d] reactive reselling

27. A voluntary acceptance of ______ concept is desirable for the long run survival of a private enterprise.

a] selling concept

b] marketing concept

c] societal concept

d] product concept

28. ______ approach believes that a satisfied consumer is the best advisor for their product.

a] Marketing concept

b] Societal concept

c] Product concept

d] Selling concept

29. Improving societies well being is the core aspect of ______ .

a] selling concept

b] marketing concept

c] product concept

d] societal concept

30. Emphasizing on consumers wants is a core aspect of ______.

a] marketing

b] selling

c] distribution

d] promotion

31. In export marketing the emphasis is on ______.

a] creating a global demand

b] expanding the market size by exporting to other countries

c] diversifying into new market

d] establishing the subsidiaries in other countries.

32. I am Philips I am Tomorrow is an example of ______

a] focused theme

b] achievement Orientation theme

c] identification theme

d] new product theme

33. 'First frost free fridge in India– Videocon', ad is an example of ______.

a] USP based ad

b] utility based ad

c] status appeal ad

d] competitive assessment ad

34. 'Tandurusti ki raksha karta hai Lifebuoy' campaign is an example of ______.

a] brand image

b] brand personality

c] brand equity

d] brand extension

35. Preparing ad budget at par with the expenditure of competitors is an example of ______.

a] Competitive parity method

b] All you can afford

c] Incremental method

d] Ad objective method

36 'Neighbour's envy owners pride- Onida' is an example of ______.

a] curiosity

b] greed

c] envy

d] novelty

37. Eureka Fibres Ltd offering a reward of mentioning the names of highly successful sales person in the 'Hall of Fame' is an example of ______.

a] cash incentive

b] bonus

c] recognition

d] perquisite

38. Buy Aristocrat and get a Philips walkman of Rs. 500/- free is an example of ______.

a] Free offer b] Coupon

c] Discount d] Free sample

39. When a firm delegates the task of selling goods abroad to an outside agency it is ______.

a] direct exporting

b] licensing

c] franchising

d] indirect exporting

40. A company assigns the right to undertake production locally by using its patent to a local company is called ______.

a] direct export b] franchising
c] joint venture d] licencing

41. An enterprise formed by an international business company sharing ownership & control with a local company in the foreign country is ______.

a] assembly
b] franchising
c] joint venture
d] contract manufacturing

42. When a company arranges to have its products manufactured by an independent local company it is called as ______.

a] contract manufacturing
b] joint venture
c] assembly
d] licensing

43. When consumers insist on having a particular brand and are willing to search and wait for it is ______.

a] brand recognition
b] brand loyalty
c] brand equity
d] brand insistance

44. The producers who believe that consumers need low priced products hence they should concentrate on efficient & extensive production, actually adopt to ______.

a] production concept
b] product concept
c] selling concept
d] marketing concept

45. A manufacturer of biscuits who concentrates on product ingredients and its appearance than consumers expectations believes in ______.

a] marketing concept

b] societal concept

c] selling concept

d] product concept

46. The marketers who believe that consumers on their own will not buy product, unless the organization undertakes aggressive sales and promotional efforts adopts______.

a] marketing concept

b] selling concept

c] societal concept

d] product concept

47. The organization that believes that needs and wants of consumers are the guiding spirit of an organizations philosophy adopt to ______.

a] societal approach

b] marketing approach

c] selling approach

d] product approach

48. This approach believes that marketing is not a business activity alone but must take into account social needs too.

a] marketing concept

b] selling concept

c] product concept

d] societal concept

49. The Howard sheth model deals with ______.

a] market research

b] sales analysis

c] consumer behavior

d] advertising effectiveness

50. Micosia model tries to establish the relationship between

a] a firm & its consumers

b] the firm & economy

c] the firm & market

d] the firm & its competitors

51. The book 'Competitive Advantage of Nations' is authored by _______.

a] Michael Porter

b] Peter Drucker

c] Thomas J. Waterman

d] Robert Frost

52. Credit rating of dealers can help _______.

a] deciding strategic treatment for dealers

b] measuring performance of dealers

c] market standing of dealers

d] deciding no. of dealers per territory

53. Market cost analysis can be a useful technique for _______.

a] controlling performance of sales persons

b] measure & analysis of profits from different product category

c] controlling cost & ensure cost related performance

d] offering variety of benefits to the firm

54. Marketing efficiency of a firm can be tested by applying a technique called _______.

a] Marketing audit

b] Marketing cost analysis

c] Market share analysis

d] M.B.O.

55. The product structured marketing organizations adds a new dimension to ______.

a] line & staff marketing organization

b] functional marketing organization

c] territory oriented organization

d] complex structure organization

56. Complex structure marketing organizations usually are ______.

a] single product multi territory organization

b] multi product – multi territory organization

c] multiple layers of authorities

d] a multinational with business in many countries

57. The task of setting marketing objectives is principally assigned to ______.

a] Marketing Officer

b] President of the firm

c] Board of Directors

d] Marketing Chief

58. Budgetary control for a marketing manager presupposes

a] ROI

b] RNOW

c] Cost per product

d] Costs & profits associated with each product

59. The dark continent in marketing is a concept coined by ______.

a] Philip Kotler

b] Peter Drucker

c] W.J. Stanton

d] J. Levitt

60. **The major indicator of Brand equity is ______.**
    a] market position
    b] consumer preference
    c] market share
    d] usership of the brand

61. **When a firm has several brands under same product category it is called ______.**
    a] Brand proliferation
    b] Brand equity
    c] Brand extension
    d] Family branding

62. **The products purchased for reselling & remarketing are ______.**
    a] Business goods
    b] Consumer goods
    c] Convenience goods
    d] Utilities

63. **An unbranded and undifferentiated commodity is called as ______.**
    a] Customized product
    b] Augmented product
    c] Customized product
    d] Generic product

64. **When a product shall be promoted & positioned after carrying out all technological & economic improvements under competitive conditions. It is a ______.**
    a] Generic product
    b] Customized product
    c] Potential product
    d] Augmented product

65. **To work out a broad based futuristic estimate ______ is used.**
   a] Expert's opinion method
   b] Surveyor's method
   c] Jury method
   d] Delphi method

66. **The demand influenced by economic cycles is called as ______.**
   a] derived demand
   b] inelastic demand
   c] specific demand
   d] market demand

67. **A buyer guided by norms of utility cost & quality is called as ______.**
   a] rational buyer
   b] purposive buyer
   c] differentiated buyer
   d] intelligent buyer

68. **"Diffusion of innovations" is a book written by______.**
   a] Erica Jones
   b] William Stanton
   c] Everrelt Rogger
   d] David Akar

69. **The model that believes that there are input stimuli & unknown varieties that influence the buyers behaviour is popularly termed as ______ .**
   a] Howard Sheth model
   b] Nicosic model
   c] Learning model
   d] Economic model

70. The fundamental unique & unbeatable strength of the firm is ______.

a] Corporate image

b] Company assets

c] Core competence

d] Inbuilt potential

71. A durable competitive advantage that can offer a unique strength to the firm is ______.

a] Brand building

b] Competitive advantage

c] Value addition

d] Benchmark

72. The value chain concept is given by ______.

a] Tom Peters

b] Michael Porter

c] Theodor Levitt

d] Chi-Nakane

73. When a major part of the market dislikes the product and may even pay a price to avoid it, such a the situation is called as ______.

a] Irregular demand

b] Full demand

c] Unwholesome demand

d] Negative demand

74. When there are organized efforts to discourage the consumption of the products the nature of demand is called as ______.

a] over full demand

b] latent demand

c] declining demand
d] unwholesome demand

75. When in the market consumers may share a strong need that can not be satisfied by any existing product, the demand pattern is called as ______.

a] latent demand
b] no demand
c] declining demand
d] irregular demand

76. Companies selling mass consumer goods and services are dealing in _______.

a] global market
b] consumer market
c] business market
d] governmental market

77. A cluster of complementary products and services that are closely related in the minds of consumers forms_______.

a] market place
b] meta market
c] target market
d] integrated market

78. The customer value triad comprises of ______.

a] cost, price and profit
b] satisfaction, value and utility
c] quality, service and price
d] benefits, costs and utility

79. A marketing net work consists of ______.

a] all departments within the co.

b] all kinds of customers.

c] customers, employees and dealers

d] all Government department affecting Co. business.

80. The task environment includes ______.

a] all kinds of customers of the Co.

b] all immediate factors involved in producing, distributing and promoting.

c] all types of channels of distribution.

d] only the government agencies.

81. The marketing programme emphasizes on______.

a] set of marketing tools to be used.

b] design marketing network.

c] tour of marketing.

d] decision on mix marketing tools to be used.

82. The concept that believes that, consumers will favour products that offer most quality performance or innovative feature is ______.

a] production concept

b] marketing concept

c] selling concepts

d] product concept

83. The concept that emphasizes on the principle putting people first is ______.

a] marketing concept

b] selling concept

c] product concept

d] production concept.

84. The present value of stream of future profits expected over the customers life time purchase is ______.

a] customers for life

b] customer relationship management

c] customer life time value

d] customer profitability analysis.

85. A part of large corporation having its own different business and set of competitors is termed as ______.

a] subsidiary unit

b] holding Co.

c] SBU

d] joint Venture

86. An area of buyers need or potential interest in which company can perform profitably is ______.

a] marketing opportunity

b] business opportunity

c] growth share matrix

d] industry demand

87. The set of consumers who are buying the company's product is ______.

a] target market

b] potential market

c] penetrated market

d] total market

88. ______ is a sales goal set for a product or brand representative.

a] Target market

b] Sales quota

c] Sales projection

d] Estimated sales

89. The index of brand sales to category sales is ______.

a] brand development index

b] market index

c] sales index

d] market share index

90. The demand decided by monitoring the buying pattern of ultimate consumers is ______.

a] market demand

b] fluctuating demand

c] professional demand

d] derived demand.

91. The demand for which business goods/services tends to be volatile due to market conditions is ______.

a] fluctuating demand

b] variable demand

c] complex demand

d] concentrated demand.

92. The products that have low value and cost to the customers are ______.

a] bottle neck products

b] strategic products

c] leverage products

d] routine products

93. Products that have wish value and cost to the customers but involve little risk of supply are ______.

a] routine products

b] strategic products

c] leverage products

d] bottle neck products.

94. Products that have low value and cost but involve risk in buying are ______.

a] strategic products

b] bottle neck product

c] routine products

d] leverage products.

95. The approach to cost reduction in which components are studied to redesign for standardization.

a] Product value analysis

b] product cost analysis

c] cost benefit analysis

d] product utility analysis.

96. The condition of blanket contract on the supplier is ______.

a] to maintain routine supply

b] to acquire goods for manufacturer.

c] to supply as needed.

d] that buyers computer automatically sends order.

97. The market that consists of hospitals, prisons schools, charitable institutions is called______.

a] N.G.O. market

b] Formal market

c] Institutional market

d] Service market

98. ______ is a market where a single firm controls supply/production side of the market.

a] Oligopoly

b] Monopoly

c] Oligarchy

d] Monopsny

99. When the same product is sold at different rates in different territories it is called as______.

a] price discrimination

b] discriminated market

c] gray market

d] marginal market

100. The fundamental service benefit for which a customer is buying a product is______.

a] core benefit

b] basic benefit

c] intrinsic benefit

d] ultimate benefit

101. A product that exceeds customers expectations due to value addition is ______.

a] basic product

b] core product

c] expected product

d] augmented product

102. Product that surpasses all possible augmentations and transformations is called______.

a] potential product

b] basic product

c] expected product

d] augmented product

103. Tangible goods that can be used many times are______.

a] non durable goods

b] durable goods

c] services

d] basic goods

104. Goods that customers usually purchase frequently with minimum efforts are_______.

a] convenience goods

b] shopping goods

c] specialty goods

d] unsought goods.

105. The abstract goals consumers are trying to satisfy with the brand are _______.

a] brand equity

b] brand image

c] brand value

d] brand essence

106. Brands that arrive with products or services that are difficult to differentiate can be termed as _______.

a] image brands

b] experimental brands

c] new brands

d] brand variant

107. Brands that involve the consumers beyond simply acquiring products are _______.

a] experimental brands

b] multi brand

c] image brand

d] functional brand

108. The statement that motivates geographically dispersed employees to work independently and yet collectively to achieve organizational goal is _______.

a] objective b] vision

c] goals d] mission

109. Buying a new CD shirt at a price double the normal price of a shirt is satisfying _______.

a] functional needs

b] hedonic needs

c] utilitarian needs

d] safety needs

110. Prudential-ICICI using a rock to indicate security is an example of

a] symbolism

b] values

c] hidden needs satisfaction

d] positioning

111. 'Wills made for each other' ad of wills is an example of _______.

a] learning process

b] positioning of the product

c] classical conditioning

d] associative learning

112. What usually directs a consumer behavior towards attaining his / her needs is a _______ .

a] stimuli

b] motive

c] need

d] desire

113. When consumers receive information most relevant to their needs it is called _______ .

a] perceptual needs

b] perceptual vigilance

c] perceptual equilibrium

d] perceptual defense

114. __________causes decision risk resulting in ineffective decision.

a] Information overload

b] Information gap

c] Information search

d] Information matrix

115. Which theory states that, people seek to achieve balance between their thoughts & feelings ?

a] Fish bone attribute model

b] Heider balance theory

c] B.C.B model

d] Four star model

116. A passive process of information used in brand processing & brand evaluation choice is _______.

a] inertia

b] id

c] ritual

d] superego

117. A group of quantitative techniques that seeks to position various brands on a map is ______.

a] micro marketing

b] micro branding

c] micro positioning

d] perceptual mapping

118. The diagram of a network of communications among individuals is _______.

a] psychogram

b] cybernetics

c] value graph

d] socio gram

119. Which values are the ultimate purchasing goals of the consumers ?

a] terminal values

b] ego

c] super ego

d] status values.

120. Manufacturer's marketing and distribution efficiency becomes the decisive factor at ______.

a] Introduction stage

b] Growth stage

c] Maturity stage

d] Slow down stage

121. The company has to invest heavily in promotion and wait for reward from market development in ______.

a] Pioneering stage

b] Growth stage

c] Maturity stage

d] Decline stage

122. MIS should be ______.

a] user oriented

b] economical

c] fast

d] all the above

123. In MIS reports in specific situations are known as______.

a] triggered reports

b] situational reports

c] specific reports

d] demand reports

124. Cannibalized income is the________income on other products of the company resulting from adding new product to the line.

a] reduced

b] additional

c] gross

d] supplementary

125. The extent of market testing is not influenced by the ______.

a] investment cost

b] time pressure

c] advertising cost

d] research cost

126. A distinctive segment of the environment in which the firm does or may want to do business is known as ______.

a] strategic business area

b] fly-area

c] cover area

d] business environment

127. 'Job-Shop specialist' firm refers to the firm which ______.

a] specialises at some vertical level of production distribution value chain

b] specialises in serving one type of end-use customers

c] customizes its products for individual customers

d] limits it selling to one or a few major customers

128. A marketing leader doesn't face the challenge of ______.

a] expanding the total market

b] segmenting the total market

c] protecting the market share

d] expanding the market share

129. A group of diverse but related items that function in a compatible manner is known as______.

a] product system

b] product family

c] product mix

d] product line

130. Consumers perception that many brand are equivalent is_______.

a] brand equity

b] brand ladder

c] brand battle

d] brand parity

131. Brand dilution refers to_______.

a] brand failure

b] multi brand situation

c] none-association with other similar products by consumers

d] non-acceptance or switching of brand by consumer.

132. Credence equalities are the characteristics that the buyer:

a] finds hard to evaluate even after consumption

b] can evaluate before purchase

c] can not evaluate of before purchase

d] can evaluate any time

133. When a product satisfies consumer wants economically it is said to have_______.

a] demand

b] utility

c] economy

d] functional application

134. In terms of goods and services, the function of marketing is to ....

a] plan market

b] create demand

c] price determination

d] distribute product

135 Not all products can be treated in the same way. Thus ________ of appropriate blending of number of elements called four P's ensure success.

a] utility concept

b] the marketing mix concept

c] the market mix concept

d] market research concept

136. The choice of a product is, among other things, based on _______.

a] attitudes

b] beliefs

c] personality

d] all of these

137. The original equipment market is _______.

a] any market for new products

b] made up of products that will be used in the manufacture

c] a group of collectors

d] limited to automotive industries

138. _________competition comes from marketers of directly similar products

a] Substitute

b] Brand

c] Buyer's purchasing power

d] Generic

139. As a part of ________ many organization perform a SWOT assessment

a] defining organizational mission

b] setting organizational objectives

c] selecting appropriate strategies

d] situation analysis

140. __________ refers to a product's image in relation to directly competitive products marketed by the same company

a] Branding

b] Positioning

c] Packaging

d] Advertising

141. __________ advantage refers to any feature of an organization or brand perceive by customers to be desirable and different from those of the competitor

a] Relative

b] Competitive

c] Differential

d] Situational

142. Order processing subsystem of physical distribution system is a procedure for __________orders

a] receiving b] landing

c] filling d] receiving, landing & filling

143. After raising a product's price, some organizations experience a considerable increase in sales this situation is called as –

a] latent demand

b] kinked demand

c] inverse demand

d] expected demand

144. A ________ is the part of a product that carries information about the product and the seller

a] level

b] press note

c] brand

d] trade mark

145. Product mix ________ is carried out either by eliminating on entire line or by simplifying the assortment within a line.

a] expansion

b] contraction

c] alteration

d] shuffling

146. ________ is to add a new product line to the company's present assortment.

a] Line extension

b] Base extension

c] Product extension

d] Mix extension

147. A/An ________ is a new product that the customer in not yet aware of –

a] unsought good

b] invention

c] addition

d] product expansion

148. A________ is a distinctive manner of constructions or presentation in art, product or endeavor.

a] fashion b] style

c] trend d] wave

149. __________ is the ability to influence or determine the behaviour of another channel member.

a] Channel control

b] Channel conflict

c] Channel contract

d] Channel power

150. "Vimal" is having its seal on "Aerial" it is an example of _______.

a] joint advertisement

b] equal contribution advertisement

c] tying contract

d] joint deal

151. Usually real objections by the prospective buyers should be dealt with_______

a] when raised

b] at a later date

c] by sidestepping them

d] no reaction

152. The prospective technique in which the sales person calls on each member of a relatively homogenous group of prospects is called _______ .

a] pioneering

b] cold canvass

c] endless chain

d] center of influence

153. The main short-run purpose of the follow-up is to _______

a] make additional sales

b] find out whether the prospect's friends would be interested in the product

c] as certain whether the buyer is satisfied
d] none of the above

154. In estimated total market potential, the total population referred as is ______.

a] Suspect pool
b] Prospect pool
c] Hot-prospect pool
d] Average pool.

155. The act of establishing and communicating the products key distinctive benefits in the market is referred as______.

a] Market segmentation
b] Market targeting
c] Market positioning
d] Market featuring

156. When the consumer preferences are scattered throughout the space it is termed as ______.

a] Heterogeneous preferences
b] Diffused preference
c] Clustered preference
d] Junk preferences

157. Consumers loyal to two or three brands are known as______.

a] Hard care loyals
b] Split loyals
c] Shifting loyals
d] Switchers

158. The difference which cannot be easily copied by competitors is known as______.

a] Preemptive difference

b] Distinctive difference

c] Superior difference

d] Important difference

159. In the fashion life cycle, emulation stage is the stage which is ranked as ______.

a] first

b] second

c] third

d] fourth.

160. A group of diverse but related items that function in a compatible manner is known as ______.

a] Product system

b] Product family

c] Product mix

d] Product line.

161. Line-extension trap refers to ______.

a] Product line failure risk

b] Chance that the brand name will lose its specific meaning

c] Innovation in product line.

d] Product line filling in.

162. To approach the understanding of a consumer market, one should have a knowledge of ______.

a] age factors

b] personal interests

c] income levels

d] all of these.

163. Marketing organisation should be ______.

a] static system

b] dynamic system

c] isolated from other departments

d] none of these.

164. A marketing organisation should be developed around the needs of______.

a] present customers

b] prospective customers

c] neither of these

d] both of these.

165. Which of the following should be included in the function of a marketing organisation?

a] The establishment of policy

b] The development of new products

c] The identification of market

d] All of these.

166. Within functionally organised marketing department, which function are under the direction of the marketing director?

a] Advertising

b] Sales

c] Marketing research

d] All of these.

167. The risk of product obsolescence, changing economic conditions, and price changes can only be handled through

a] insurance

b] good management

c] hedging

d] reduction of elimination of the risk.

168. Which, of the following firms is most likely to use hedging as a method of handling risk?

a] A manufacturer of soyabean oil

b] A major diary

c] A major airline

d] A construction firm.

169. The requirements of insurable risk include all the following statements except _______.

a] the loss must be measurable and predictable

b] the risks must be numerous

c] the risks must be spread out

d] the loss must be unintentional

170. The basic insurance principle which makes it uneconomical to overinsure one's property is _______.

a] the law of large numbers

b] insurable risk

c] indemnity

d] coinsurance

171. Of the following, which is the most popular and widely used form of life insurance?

a] Term

b] Straight-life

c] Endowment

d] Limited-payment life.

172. Of the following, the type of life insurance which provides for the greatest saving features is _______.

a] term

b] straight-life

c] endowment

d] limited-payment life.

173. Of the following, the statement that best expresses the basic idea behind the marketing concept is ______.

a] produce the best possible product

b] produce the cheapest possible product

c] try to reduce the cost of marketing

d] keep the consumer foremost in mind

174. The concept of modern marketing puts________ at the beginning and end of the marketing cycle.

a] sellers

b] buyers

c] producers

d] retailers

175. Distribution involves________.

a] storage

b] the transfer of title

c] physical movement

d] all of the above.

176. Manufactures who sell to wholesalers rather than directly to retailers can.

a] dispense with advertising their products

b] dispense with personal selling

c] operate with a small amount of capital

d] increase their cost of marketing.

177. In general, the advantage of using rail freight is greatest when________ is the most important factor.

a] cost

b] speed

c] geographical coverage

d] safety

178. Wholesalers and middlemen who do not take title to the goods they sell are know as _______.

a] cash-and carry wholesalers

b] desk jobbers

c] agents and brokers

d] rack jobbers.

179. Distribution involves those activities of getting goods from the producer to the_______.

a] agent

b] wholesaler

c] retailer

d] ultimate user.

180. Most consumers want _______.

a] small quantities of many products

b] small quantities of few products

c] large quantities of few products

d] large quantities of many products

181. The channel typical of many products sold through chain stores and large department stores is _______.

a] manufacturer-retailer-consumer

b] manufacturer-consumer

c] manufacturer-wholesaler-retailer-consumer

d] manufacturer-agent-wholesaler-retailer-consumer.

182. One advantage of using public warehouses rather than private warehouses is that _______.

a] public warehouses are usually cheaper

b] public warehouses provide greater security for goods in storage c] public warehouses issue warehouses receipts which may be used as collateral

d] public warehouses are usually single storied while private warehouses are usually multi-storied.

183. A type of salesperson whose main job is one of introducing new products to dealers and retailers is referred at a ______.

a] retailer

b] merchandising salesperson

c] sales engineer

d] pioneer products salesperson

184. Most salespersons feel that the two hard steps or stages of the sales process are the ______.

a] pre approach and post approach

b] approach and demonstration

c] contact and object

d] approach and closing

185. The least important human sense in terms of sales demonstrations is ______.

a] sight b] hearing

c] smell d] touch.

186. The main short-run purpose of the follow-up is to

a] make additional sales

b] find out whether the prospect's friends would be interested in the product

c] ascertain whether the buyer is satisfied.

d] none of the above.

187. Demonstrations should be made at ______interview.

a] the very beginning of

b] the close of

c] any time that is necessary during

d] none of the above.

188. When new products do not succeed, the explanation is often _______.

a] mismanagement

b] consumer rejection

c] economic fluctuation

d] marketing weakness.

189. The amount of satisfaction the purchaser expects to get from the purchase is reflected in _______.

a] frequency of purchase

b] scarcity of the item

c] price

d] size

190. When a country decides to produce goods that will bring it the greatest advantage, it is accepting the principle of _______.

a] absolute advantage

b] competitive advantage

c] comparative advantage

d] economic advantage.

191. A firm's source to finance its day-to-day operations is usually satisfied by _______.

a] receipts from sales

b] loans from banks

c] selling stocks

d] none of the above.

192. In terms of goods and services, the function of marketing is to______ demand

a] plan

b] create

c] price

d] promote.

193. Not all products can be treated in the same way. The appropriate blending of number of elements to ensure success is ______ .

a] utility

b] the marketing concept

c] the marketing mix

d] market research.

194. A general perspective of attitude the marketer has toward the customer is known as ______ .

a] Market mission

b] Market philosophy

c] Market objective

d] Market goal.

195. Branding is concerning with__________component of four 'P'.

[a] Promotion

[b] Place

[c] Price

[d] Product

196. The__________stimulates the purchase at the critical moment when the consumer is making a choice.

[a] Brand

[b] Advertisement

[c] Package

[d] Company image

197. An unobservable inner force that stimulates and compels a behavioral response is______.

[a] Motive

[b] Need

[c] Attitude

[d] None of these.

198. Narrowly focused markets that are defined by some special interest are termed as______.

[a] Target markets

[b] Mass markets

[c] Niche markets

[d] Undifferentiated markets.

199. A products position is located in the minds of______.

[a] advertiser

[b] salesman

[c] consumer

[d] all of these

200. For a brand, the idea of accumulating a reservoir of goodwill & good impressions is called as ______.

[a] Brand image

[b] Brand personality

[c] Brand differentiation

[d] Brand equity

201. An exercise in which one describes everything that comes in mind while thinking of a word or an image, is______.

[a] Idea generation

[b] Visualization

[c] Free association

[d] Thinking

202. A rational, informational message that emphasizes a strong argument, and calls for action is known as______.

[a] Lecture

[b] Hard sell

[c] Soft sell

[d] Direct sell

ANSWERS

1) b) augmented product
2) c) wheel of retailing theory
3) a) weakest link theory
4) d) wholly owned subsidiary
5) b) Variable leader pricing
6) a) Usage rate segmentation
7) a) Universal product code
8) a) USP
9) c) Umbrella pricing
10) c) Undifferentiated segmentation
11) a) projection
12) b) trading area
13) b) time utility
14) c) tactical planning
15) b) swap market
16) a) grocery store
17) a) sunk cost
18) a) validity
19) a) repeat purchase
20) c) status quo pricing
21) d) speciality discount store
22) b) societal forces
23) c) Safety needs
24) a) risk aversion pricing
25) c) resale price maintenance
26) c) repositioning
27) c) societal concept
28) a) marketing concept
29) d) societal concept
30) b) selling

31) c) diversifying into new market
32) c) identification theme
33) a) USP based
34) a) brand image
35) a) Competitive parity method
36) c) envy
37) c) recognition
38) a) Free offer
39) c) franchising
40) d) licensing
41) c) joint venture
42) a) contract manufacturing
43) b) Brand loyalty
44) a) Production concept
45) d) product concept
46) b) selling concept
47) b) marketing approach
48) d) societal concept
49) c) consumer behavior
50) c) The firm & market
51) a) Michael Porter
52) c) market standing of dealers
53) a) controlling performance of sales persons
54) a) Marketing audit
55) c) territory oriented organization
56) b) multi product multi territory organizations
57) d) Marketing Chief
58) d) Costs and profits associated with each product
59) c) W.J. Stnnton
60) d) usership of the brand
61) a) Brand proliferation
62) d) business goods

63) d) generic product
64) c) Potential product
65) d) Delphi method
66) d) market demand
67) a) Rational buyer
68) c) Everett Rogger
69) b) Nicosia model
70) c) Core competence
71) a) brand building
72) b) Michael Porter
73) c) unwholesome demand
74) d) Unwholesome demnad
75) a) latent demand
76) b) consumer market
77) b] meta market
78) c) quality service price
79) c) customers, employees & dealesrs
80) b) all immediate factors involving in producing distribute & marketing
81) a] set of marketing tools to be used
82) d] product concept
83) a] marketing concept
84) c] customer life time value
85) c] SBU
86) b] business opportunity
87) a) target market
88) b] sales quota
89) a) Brand development index
90) a) market demand.
91) b) variable demand
92) d] routine products
93) c] products

94) b] prodcuts
95) d) product utility analysis
96) c] to supply as needed
97) c] institutional market
98) b] monopoly
99) b] discriminated market
100) a] core benefit
101) d] augmented product
102) a] potential product
103) b] durable goods
104) a] convenience goods
105) b] brand image
106) d] brand variant
107) c] image brand
108) d) mission
109) b] hedonic needs
110) a] symbolism
111) d] associative learning
112) a] stimuli
113) c] Perpectual equilirium
114) a] Information overload
115) b] Heiders balance theory
116) a] inertia
117) d] perceptual mapping
118) b] cybernetics
119) a] terminal values
120) c] maturity stage
121) a] pioneering stage
122) d] all the above
123) a] triggered reports
124) b] additional
125) b] time pressure

126) a] strategic business area
127) b] specialises in serving one typeof end use customers
128) a] expanding the total market
129) b] product family
130) d] brand parity
131) b] multibrand situation
132) d] can evaluate any time
133) d] unctional application
134) b] create demand
135) b] the marketing mix concept
136) d] all of these
137) b] made of products that will be used in mention
138) d] generic
139) a] defining organizaitonal mission
140) b] positioning
141) b) competitive
142) c] filling
143) b] kinked demand
144) d) trade mark
145) b) contraction
146) c) rpoduct extension
147) a) unsought good
148) d) wave
149) d) channel power
150) a) joint advertisement
151) a) when raised
152) d) center of influence
153) b) find whehter prospects friend is intersted in product
154) c) Hot-prospect pool
155) d) market featuring
156) b) diffused preference
157) b) split loyals

158) a) preemptive difference
159) b) second
160) c) Product mix
161) b) Chance that the brand name will lose meaning
162) d) all of these
163) b) dynamic system
164) b) prespective customers
165) d) all of these
166) d) all of these
167) b) good management
168) a) A manufacturer of soyabean oil
169) d) the loss must be unintentional
170) b) in surable risk.
171) c) Endowment
172) d) limited payment life
173) d) keep the foremost premost in mind
174) b) buyers
175) d) all of the above
176) b) dispense with personal selling
177) a) cost
178) c) cash of carry wholesalers
179) d) ultimat user
180) a) small quantities of many products
181) a) manufacturer retailer consumer
182) c) public warehouses issues warehouses receipts which may be used as collateral
183) b) merchandising salesperson
184) a) preapproach & post approach
185) c) smell
186) c) ascertain whether the boyer is satisfied
187) a) the very beginning of
188) b) consumer rejection.

189) a) frequency of purchase
190) d) economic advantage
191) a) receipts from sles
192) b) create
193) c) the marketing mix
194) b) market philosophy
195) a) promotion
196) c) package
197) a) Motive
198) c) Niche market
199) c) consumer
200) b) brand personality
201) b) visualization
202) b) hardsell

2

ADVERTISING

1. **Advertising associated with presentation of ideas & social issues of several importance is ____________.**
   a] article advertising
   b] creative advertising
   c] social advertising
   d] advocacy advertising

2. **A delayed effect of advertising on sales during a subsequent time period ____________.**
   a] carry over effect
   b] system effect
   c] delayed effect
   d] stimuli effect

3. **An index calculated by taking the percentage of brands total sales that occur in a given market compared to percentage of total population in the market ____________.**
   a] carry over effect
   b] brand development index
   c] category development index
   d] clutter index

4. **Specialized Services provided by firms to companies such as package design research etc. are called as ___________.**
   a] secondary services
   b] associative services
   c] collateral services
   d] augmented services

5. **Command head line is ___________.**
   a] the most important headline
   b] headline with new idea
   c] headline that orders to do something
   d] headline that creates interest

6. **Setting advertisement budget based on matching the absolute level of competition is ___________.**
   a] Target based method
   b] Comparative parity method
   c] Quota method
   d] Utility based method

7. **The advertisement strategy that decides what an advertising message will say to target audience is ___________.**
   a] creative idea strategy
   b] direct message strategy
   c] focussed message strategy
   d] need based message strategy

8. **Consumer reactions tests to advertisements that are conducted under natural viewing situation is termed as ___________.**
   a] Target audience test
   b] Critical factor tests
   c] Field tests
   d] Response tests

9. A tendency to evaluate one attribute or aspect of stimulus to distort reactions to other is __________.

a] Comparative effect

b] Halo effect

c] Hirearchy effect

d] image effect

10. Ratio used to describe potential of a market ___________.

a] Consumer ratio

b] Index number

c] Potential ratio

d] Market response ratio

11. A document that spells objectives, strategies and tactics of reaching a target audience __________.

a] sales plan

b] activity plan

c] media plan

d] target plan

12. The specific publication or programme to carry an advertising message is ___________.

a] media vehicle

b] exhibit

c] publication syndicate

d] advertisement document

13. Perceptual map is ___________.

a] map of target market

b] map of segmented consumer packets

c] map of perceptions of brands as received by consumers

d] map of specific sales territory

14. Primary effect means ___________.

a] information presented in the advertising Message will be most likely to be remembered

b] the first advertisement is remembered for long

c] the first line of ad is most important

d] product campaign must consider primary needs of the consumer

15. Research based on criteria that cannot be quantified like attributes is ___________.

a] quantitative research

b] qualitative research

c] activity research

d] action research

16. A measurement used to determinc television audience___________.

a] Television index

b] Television response

c] Rating point

d] Popularity index

17. The approach that believes that arguments presented at the end of ad message is more powerful and hence more likely to be remembered is termed as___________.

a] media effect

b] Rrccency effect

c] reinforcement

d] recall effect

18. The process in which consumers choose whether or not to be exposed to media & message

a] Selective exposure

b] Selective attention

c] Selective reactivity

d] Selective perception

19. Consumers remember only some part of information but not all of it due to ____________.

a] Selective exposure

b] Selective attention

c] Selective reactivity

d] Selective perception

20. .... used in an ad with dramatisation of real life situation, where the product proves solution to the problem.

a] Sleeper effect

b] Slice of life

c] Rational appeal

d] Primary effect

21. When favorable thoughts are generated towards message presenter it is termed as ____________.

a] source bolsters

b] source derogations

c] sleeper effect

d] primacy effect

22. An ad designed to evolve curiosity in a product without showing it is ____________.

a] Trade advertising

b] Transformational advertising

c] Transit advertising

d] Teaser advertising

23. Transit ad. is an advertisement targeted to audience:

a] Exposed to ads on buses, planes & trains

b] Exposed to ads in theaters

c] Exposed to ads on TV

d] Exposed to ads on walls

24. Zapping is the technique ___________.

a] to change the TV channels to avoid seeing commercials

b] to view only select ads on TV

c] to influence audience through a specific TV screened a quite frequently

d] intentional display of a particular ad at an regular interval.

25. An advertisement promotes 'diet coke' for women is an example of ___________.

a] Persuasion

b] Information

c] Promotion

d] Idea generation

26. Advertisement of a electronic blood pressure measuring device is directed at ___________.

a] industrial users

b] professionals

c] commercial users

d] members of business organization

27. Advertisement of Chirag Din shirts appearing in Times of India serves

a] national market

b] regional market

c] local market

d] specialized segments

28. TATA steel is a 70 years old reputed name in the market which indicates ___________.

a] brand loyalty

b] brand equity

c] brand image

d] brand reputation

29. PARLEY FRUITY an addition to Parley biscuits and confectionary is an example of ___________.

a] brand addition

b] family branding

c] brand extension

d] brand equity

30. An ad suggesting "call this toll free number" is an example of ___________.

a] demand stimulation

b] direct response ad

c] promotional campaign

d] delayed response ad

31. "Introduction of light beer- Kingfisher" is an example of ___________.

a] product new in the industry

b] product new for the mankind

c] product new for the product category

d] product new in the product class

32. Introduction of EURO-II emission level car is an example of ___________.

a] new product due to government resolution

b] new product due to technological changes

c] variation in product life cycle

d] new product due to change in consumer demand

33. A marketing research technique adopted to identify consumers perception about competitors product is _______.

a] product research

b] product audit

c] product augmentation

d] product development

34. Van Heusen shirts offered at high price tag with aggressive promotional campaign is an example of ____________.

a] skimming price

b] penetration price

c] administer price

d] churning price

35. Idea generation with the help of particular usage/ needs analysis and surveys of attitude is an example of __________.

a] category analysis

b] active search

c] competition analysis

d] customer analysis

36. Examining changing social trends and technologies to develop a new product is an example of ____________. .

a] concept testing

b] category analysis

c] competitive analysis

d] customer analysis

37. 'Shoppers stop' advertise to promote ____________.

a] a specific brand

b] a specific product line

c] a specific corporate house

d] to attract audience to their store

38. The advertisement "value for your money" is aimed at ____________.

a] price of the product

b] purchasing power

c] value addition

d] consumer satisfaction

39. Ray-ban goggles advertising featuring a top hollywood star signifies ____________.

a] status symbol

b] symbolic value

c] social value

d] monetary value

40. 'Johnson Baby Powder' now available for Rs. 25/- is an advertisement stating____________.

a] emotional benefit

b] functional benefit

c] specific benefit

d] status benefit

41. 'Kalnirnay' the utility almanc ad as your companion for the whole year is an example of ____________.

a] emotional benefit

b] functional benefit

c] value addition

d] status benefit

42. 'Tata Indigo' as a car your neighbour envies is an example of ____________.

a] value addition

b] status benefit

c] emotional benefit

d] functional benefit

43. The ad having bottom line 'Diamonds are forever' is an example of ____________.

a] low involvement decision

b] high involvement decision

c] extended problem solving

d] limited problem solving

44. The emotional appeal in the ad of Titan Watches is an example of ___________.

a] extended problem solving

b] limited problem solving

c] involvement decision

d] variety seeking

45. Welcome to the abode of God the Himalayan kingdom-Himachal is an ad encashing ___________.

a] ideas

b] attitude

c] specific benefit

d] presumptions

46. 'Rangoli' the ad of Asian Paints on festive occasion of Dipawali is an example of ___________.

a] encashing the culture

b] encashing the seasonal demand

c] encashing the product features

d] encashing the concept

47. The fundamental objective of _______ is to identify those trends forces and conditions which have a potential impact on formulation of marketing strategy

a] vulnerability analysis

b] marketing analysis

c] value analysis

d] SWOT analysis

48. _______ involves analysis for the best ways to achieve competitive advantages

a] value analysis

b] gap analysis

c] bench marking

d] SWOT analysis

49. The stage in which a consumer learns about the new product and know about its benefit is ___________.

a] awareness stage

b] knowledge stage

c] decision stage

d] persuasion stage

50. A person who frequently influences other individuals attitude or overt behavior is an ___________.

a] influencer

b] innovator

c] idea generator

d] opinion maker

51. Consumers often use price factor of a product as a means to indicate their status or position in society this is termed as ___________.

a] price appeal

b] status appeal

c] value appeal

d] snob appeal

52. When a consumer conjures up in his mind a price for a product which he considers to be just it is called as____________..

a] fair price standard

b] cost price standard

c] optimum price standard

d] minimum price standard

53. _______ this function of advertising tells the market as well as consumers about the product and the brands

a] Reminding

b] Informing

c] Reassuring

d] persuading

54. _______ function of advertising tells the consumers that they have made a wise choice.

a] Reminding
b] Persuading
c] Reassuring
d] Entertainment

55. _______ involves the model process of constructing pictures of the numerous objects we see.

a] Perception
b] Persuasion
c] Retention
d] Facilitation

56. The type of ad that helps the people sympathise towards the sufferer has ___________.

a] fear appeal
b] abrasive appeal
c] agony appeal
d] numor appeal

57. The ad where the sentences fade out of memory overtime and only the brand name is remembered by the audience has ___________.

a] sympathy appeal
b] identity appeal
c] agony appeal
d] abrasive appeal

58. The method of finding out potential customers is __________.

a] prospecting
b] informing
c] hunting
d] identifying

59. A sales person who makes an unsolicited call is using the technique of ____________..

a] spotting

b] cold calling

c] influencing

d] hunting

60. The process of becoming aware of situations of adding meaningful associations is____________.

[a] perception

[b] idea

[c] desire

[d] motivation

61. The minimal difference that can be detected by any sense organ between two stimuli is the ____________.

[a] JND- Just Natural Difference

[b] basic difference

[c] additional difference

[d] instinctive difference

62. The tendency for people to judge a particular characteristics of an object in terms of their several impression is ________.

[a] perception effect

[b] image effect

[c] halo effect

[d] positional effect

63. The share of the market held by a firm or product as compared to the market share of competitors ____________.

[a] relevant market share

[b] relative market share

[c] net market share

[d] reciprocal market share

64. A straight forward lie in advertising is called ______.

a] misleading ad

b] corrective ad

c] fraudulent ad

d] false ad

65. Advertising stating durability & ease in riding a cycle is an example of ______.

a] self esteem need

b] utilitarian need

c] hedonic needs

d] safety needs

66. The science of assigning signs & symbols to objects is called as ______.

a] graphics

b] helo graphics

c] gemiotics

d] semantics

67. The appeals that are directed towards the thinking faculty of the audience are ______..

a] rational appeals

b] moral appeals

c] emotional appeals

d] humor appeals

68. N.R.S. stands for______.

a] National Readers' System

b] National Review Service

c] National Religious Service

d] National Readership Survey

69. ASCI stands for __________.

a] Advertising Social Code of India

b] Advertising Standards Council of India

c] Advertising System & Codes of India

d] Advertising Standards & Commerce of India

70. ABC Stands for ____________.

a] Actual benificers Code

b] Audit Bureau of Circulation

c] Audit Based Costing

d] Advertising & Broadcasting Council

71. The self image is the personality and character that should usually match brand image for creating effective__________.

a] ad appeals

b] brand equity

c] marketing communication

d] marketing strategy

72. When the ad emphasizes usefulness of a product then it is termed as ____________.

a] utilitarian theme

b] focused theme

c] informative theme

d] non specific theme

73. When the advertiser announces achievement to its credit to amplify the image it is ____________.

a] projective theme

b] focused theme

c] informative theme

d] achievement orientation theme

74. Institutional advertising is ___________.

a] aimed only at people in institutions

b] run only by institutions

c] designed to promote a type of product rather than a particular brand

d] designed simply to show that the firm is a good place to do business.

75. When competing firms in the same industry unite to promote their product as a whole, their advertising is best described as___________.

a] primary demand advertising

b] institutional advertising

c] indirect demand advertising

d] trade advertising

76. An outdoor billboard that says "Drink Milk for Health" is an example of ___________.

a] primary demand advertising

b] institutional advertising

c] indirect demand advertising

d] trade advertising

77. The most important advertising media today, at least in terms of total advertising investment is ___________.

a] newspaper

b] magazines

c] television

d] direct mail.

78. The most selective advertising medium geographically and qualitatively, is ___________.

a] newspaper

b] magazines

c] television

d] direct mail.

79. Which of the following is not an advantage of newspapers as an advertising medium?

a] high geographic selectivity

b] high qualitative selectivity

c] high degree of flexibility

d] relatively low cost.

80. Which of the following is not an advantage of direct mail?

a] high geographic selectivity

b] high qualitative selectivity

c] high degree of flexibility

d] relatively low cost.

81. Of the following which is not characteristics of television as an advertising medium?

a] good geographic selectivity

b] moderate qualitatively selectivity by program

c] relatively long life

d] relatively high cost.

82. Which of the following is not characteristics of magazines as an advertising medium?

a] good geographic selectivity

b] good qualitative selectivity

c] relatively long life

d] poor flexibility.

83. The biggest disadvantage of using outdoor advertising as a medium is

a] difficult in obtaining good locations

b] high cost

c] poor quality of reproduction in that size

d] limited copy.

84. The largest single source of income for agencies is ....

[a] direct payment from clients

[b] commissions from media

[c] discounts of client's products

[d] profit sharing.

85. A planned, coordinated and unified series of ads is called a ....

[a] tactic

[b] promotional survey

[c] campaign

[d] bitz.

86. Which of the following is the correct sequence of mental stages through which the buyer is led?

[a] attention, interest desire and action

[b] desire, action, attention and interest

[c] interest, desire, attention and action

[d] action, interest, desire and attention

87. Usually, real objections by the prospective buyer should be dealt with ....

[a] at a later date

[b] by side stepping them

[c] when raised

[d] not al all.

88. The word advertisement first appeared around ....

[a] 1655

[b] 1670

[c] 1700

[d] 1712

89. Advertising which creates messages through a slow accumulation of positive image is ________.

a] push-sell advertising

b] pull-sell advertising

c] soft-sell advertising

d] hard-sell advertising

90. The concept of "Brand name" was coined by ________.

a] J. Water Thompson

b] Helen & Stanely Resor

c] Claude Hopkins

d] John S. Kennedy

91. 'Status appeal' was developed first by ________.

a] Helen & Stanely Resor

b] J.W. Thompson

c] C. Hopkins

d] J.S. Kennedy.

92. The value of an idea is measured by its ________.

a] Creativity

b] Novelty

c] Originality

d] Presentation

93. Rosser Reeves proposed the concept of ________.

a] Fear appeal

b] USP

c] TRP

d] Copy

94. Professional & trade advertising corresponds to the________.

a] Consumer market

b] Marketing mix

c] Resellers market

d] Institutional market

95. A form of advertising in which the manufacturer reimburses the retailer for part or all of the retailer's advertising expenditure is ___________.

a] retail advertising

b] reimbursing advertising

c] support advertising

d] cooperative advertising

96. Customer contact is indirect in case of ___________.

a] advertising

b] sales promotion

c] direct response

d] public relations

97. An advertising agency ___________.

a] gives a product a personality

b] creates An image or memorable picture of the product

c] sets the product apart from its competitors

d] performs all the above function.

98. Which of the following is not a function of advertising agency___________.

a] Account management

b] Creative development of production

c] Media planning and buying

d] None of these

99. The appointment of one agency to handle all the advertising of a client's divisions is termed as___________.

a] Blanketing

b] Consolidation

c] Single contracting1

d] Monotonation.

100. An ad agency does not have a ______ department as a support department.

a] traffic

b] print production

c] human resources

d] none of these

101. The ability to process only certain information and avoid other stimuli is___________.

a] Selective perception

b] Selective exposure

c] Selective distortion

d] Selective retention.

102. The sales logic behind an advertising message is known as____________.

a] Claim

b] Promise

c] Selling premises

d] Message benefit.

103. An advertising problem in which an ad is so creative or entertaining that it overwhelms the product is termed as____________.

a] Superimpose

b] Vampire creativity

c] Key visual

d] Taglines.

104. A television technique where one image is added to another that is already on the screen is known as______.

a] Maximize

b] Addingles

c] Vampire image

d] Superimpose

105. Image advertising that changes the experience of buying or using a product is ___________.

a] Change advertising

b] Transformation advertising

c] Exciting advertising

d] Buy advertising

106. Transformation advertising is an example of ___________.

a] Primary advertising

b] Secondary advertising

c] Direct action advertising

d] Indirect-action advertising

107. Which option is wrong, transformation advertising ________.

a] is a big budget

b] can be used to turn around perceived negatives

c] can work for products related to unpleasant experiences

d] none of the above

108. Advertising works at ___________.

a] perception level

b] awareness level

c] persuasion level

d] all the above

109. A decision leading to the use of advertising time and space to assist in the achievement of marketing objective is known as ___________.

a] Advertising planning

b] Media selection

c] Media planning

d] Advertising execution

110. 'Aperture' is the ideal moment for exposing____________.

a] consumers to media

b] advertisement to media

c] consumer to advertising message

d] media to advertising massage

111. The percentage of advertising messages in a medium by one brand among all messages for that product or service is called as____________.

a] Share of voice

b] Media percentage

c] Media coverage

d] Brand share

112. The sum of the total exposure potential of a series of media vehicles expressed as a percentage of the audience population is referred as____________.

a] Total rating points

b] Gross rating points

c] Net rating points

d] Nominal rating points.

113. Media are compared on the basis of their relative efficiency, which means____________.

a] Cost and audience size

b] Cost of creativity

c] Creativity and audience size

d] Any of the above.

114. Media. plans are interwoven with other areas of advertising except ____________.

a] The budget

b] The target audience

c] The message demands

d] None of these

115. Network advertising schedules are dominated by__________.

a] Audience

b] Network authorities

c] Large national advertisers

d] None of these.

116. An arrangement in which a television advertiser buys commercial time from a network is termed as ____________.

a] Sponsorship

b] Participation

c] Spot announcement

d] Spot buys.

117. The disadvantage of radio is ____________.

a] flexibility is lacking

b] mental imagery

c] clutter

d] high costs.

118. The advantage of television is____________.

a] less costly

b] clutter force

c] flexibility

d] reaches large audiences.

119. A newspaper with a page size of 5to 6 columns wide and 14 inches deep is ___________.

a] Broadsheet

b] Tabloid

c] Deep sheet

d] None of the above

120. Sponsored messages that can be of any size and location within the newspaper with the exception of the editorial page is ___________.

a] classified advertising

b] supplements advertising

c] free-standing advertisements

d] display advertising

121. Preprinted advertisements that are placed loosely within the news paper is ___________.

a] supplemented advertising

b] classified advertising

c] free- standing advertising

d] delivery within news papers.

122. Traditional delivery of magazines refers to___________.

a] door hangers

b] news stands

c] delivery through professionals

d] delivery within news papers.

123. Second cover page of magazine refers to___________.

a] front cover page

b] back cover page

c] inside of front cover page

d] inside of back cover page.

124. The use of as many different stations and programs as possible to avoid duplicating the message to audience is called as ____________.

a] Dispersion

b] Multimedia

c] Deviation

d] Variation

125. Creative concept in an ad. makes the message____________.

a] Distinctive

b] Attentive

c] Memorable

d] All the above.

126. 'Cliches' in advertising means____________.

a] original idea

b] copied idea

c] relevant idea

d] empathetic idea

127. An extreme concentration on strategy is termed as_________.

a] strategy hypnosis

b] strategy concentration

c] strategy targeting

d] strategy foundation

128. An emotional message that uses mood, ambiguity, and suspense to create or response bases on feelings and attitudes is_____________.

a] hard sell

b] direct sell

c] indirect sell

d] soft sell

129. An advertising format in which spoke person describes a positive personal experience with the product is termed as____________.

a] Drama

b] Testimonial

c] Lecture

d] Script

130. Advertising text that is written from the company's point of view to extall its virtues and accomplishment is____________.

a] Bray-and boast copy

b] Add Text

c] Ad teaser copy

d] Stint copy

131. Formula writing that uses cliches, generalities, short phrases & superlatives is____________.

a] bray-and boast copy

b] add text

c] adese

d] stint copy

132. A creative concept must have ____________.

a] Relevance

b] Originality

c] Impact

d] All the above

133. Effective copy writing should not be____________.

a] informal

b] personal

c] forced

d] concise.

134. Copy does not include.......... .

[a] underlines

[b] captions

[c] taglines

[d] signatures

135. The visual element in an ad as is known as____________.

a] Art

b] Copy

c] Text

d] Script.

136. Subheads, Captions, and Slogans are included in__________.

a] Text

b] Art

c] Text

d] Script

137. Logos and signatures are the elements of____________.

a] text b] art

c] copy d] script

138. One advertising principle states that, tell as much as of the study in_______ as possible.

a] Body copy

b] Text

c] Headline

d] Tagline.

139. The ads with incomplete headline employ a psychological principle called as____________.

a] Aperture

b] Closure

c] Halfen

d] Incomplete.

140. The headlines referred as 'Blind' are____________.

a] primary
b] secondary
c] direct
d] indirect.

141. Tests of two versions of the same version ad are known as ____________.

a] Split-run tests
b] Double tests
c] Comparitive tests
d] Toll test.

142. A subhead that leads into the headline is called as____________.

a] Caption
b] Tagline
c] Overline
d] Underline

143. A subhead that leads from the headline into the body copy is termed as____________.

a] Caption
b] Overline
c] Underline
d] Tagline.

144. A memorable phrase that sums up the concept or key point of the ad is ____________.

a] Tagline
b] Caption
c] Subhead
d] Principle

145. The first element in a layout that the eye sees is___________.

a] dominance

b] focal Point

c] highlight

d] one of the above.

146. An ad in which the printed area runs to the trim of the page is___________.

a] Contrast

b] plain

c] Bleed

d] Craton

147. A point slightly above the mathematical center of a page is termed as___________.

a] Dominance center

b] Focal center

c] Lighting center

d] Optical center.

148. People who appear in television commercials are called as___________.

a] Characters

b] Hosts

c] Talent

d] Guests.

149. Computer-generated letters that move across the bottom of the screen are___________.

a] Crawl

b] Scrabbles

c] Pace

d] Props.

150. The term 'Junk Mail' refers to____________.

a] personal selling

b] direct marketing

c] indirect marketing

d] sky shopping.

151. Yellow pages advertising is an example of____________.

a] primary advertising

b] institutional advertising

c] directional advertising

d] feature advertising

152. Multisided bullet in board structure designed for public posting of messages is know as____________.

a] Kiosks

b] Billboards

c] Cutouts

d] Way bills

153. Large structure erected on highway and roads for the display of huge advertising posters__________.

a] Kiosks

b] Hoardings

c] Billboards

d] Cutouts

154. Disadvantage of outdoor advertising relates to____________.

a] impact

b] exposure

c] messaged

d] life

155. Bill boards with unusual lighting effects are known as____________.

a] Holography

b] Inflatable

c] Kiosks

d] Spectaculars.

156. A technique that produces a projected 3-D image is referred as____________.

a] Holography

b] Inflatography

c] Kinctography

d] Spectaculars.

ANSWERS

1] d] advocacy advertising

2] a] carry over effect

3] b] brand development index

4] c] collateral services

5] c] Headline that orders to do something

6] b] comparative parity method

7] a] creative idea strategy

8] c] Field tests

9] b] Halo effect

10] d] Market response ratio

11] c] media plan

12] a] media vehicle

13] c] map of perceptions od brands as received by consumers

14] a] information presented in the ad message will be most likely to be remembered

15] b] qualitative research

16] c] rating point

17] c) reinforcement

18] a] selective exposure

19] selective retention

20] b] slice of life

21] a] source bolsters

22] d) Teaser advertising

23] a] expressed to ads on buses, planes and trains

24] a] to change the T.V. channels to avoid seeing commercials

25] a] Persuasion

26] b] Professionals

27] c] Local market

28] b] brand equity

29] c] brand extension

30] b] direct response ad

31] c] product new for the product category

32] a] new product due to government resolution

33] b] product audit

34] b) penetration price

35] d] customer analysis

36] b] category analysis

37] d] to attract audience to their store

38] c] value addition

39] b] symbolic value

40] a] emotional benefit

41] b) functional benefits

42] b] status benefit

43] b] high involvement decision

44] c] involvement decision

45] b] attitude

46] a] encashing the culture

47] d] SWOT analysis

48] d] SWOT analysis

49] b] knowledge stage

50] d] opinion maker

51] d] snob appeal
52] a) fair price standard
53] a) reminding
54] b] persuading
55] a] Perception
56] c] agony appeal
57] d] abrasive appeal
58] a] prospecting
59] b] cold calling
60] a] perception
61] a) JND = just Natural Difference
62] a) perception effect
63] b] relative market share
64] b) Corrective ad
65] b) utilitarian need
66] b) helo graphics
67] a) rational appeals
68] d) National Readership survey
69] b) Advertising Standards council of India
70] b) Audit Bureau of Circulation
71] c) marketing communication
72] a) Utilitarian theme
73] d) achievement orientation theme
74] d) designed simply to show that the firm is a good place to do business
75] a) Primary demand advertising
76] a) Primary demand adversting
77] c) television
78] a) newspaper
79] c) high degree of flexibility
80] d) relatively low cast
81] c) relatively long life
82] d) poor flexibility
83] d) Limited copy

84] a) direct payment from clients
85] c) campaign
86] a) attention, interest, desire and action
87] c) when raised
88] b) 1670
89] c) soft-sell adversting
90] c) Claude Hopkins
91] d) J.S. Kenedy
92] c) originality
93] b) USP
94] c) Resellers market
95] b) reimbursing adversting
96] a) advertising
97] c) sets the product apart from its competitors
98] b) creative development of production
99] a) Blanketing
100] c) human resources
101] b) selective exposure
102] a) claim
103] a) superimpose
104] c) vampire image
105] b) transformation advertising
106] c) Direct action adverstising
107] a) is a big budget
108] d) all the above
109] d) adversising execution
110] c) Consumer to adversting message
111] a) Share of voice
112] b) Gross rating points
113] c) creativity & audience size
114] c) The message demands
115] c) large national advertisers
116] d) Spot buys

117] c) clutter
118] d) reaches large audiences
119] b) tabloid
120] c) free standing advertisements
121] c) standing advertising
122] b) Free standing adversising
123] b) back cover page
124] b) multimedia
125] c) memorable
126] c) Relevant idea
127] a) strategy hypnosis
128] a) hard sell
129] b) testimonial
130] a) Bray and Boast copy
131] d) stint copy
132] a) Relevance
133] c) Forced
134] d) Signatures
135] a) Art
136] a) Text
137] c) copy
138] a) Body copy
139] c) Halfen
140] d) Indirect
141] c) comparitive tests
142] c) overline
143] b) overline
144] a) tagline
145] b) focal point
146] c) Bleed
147] d) optical center
148] d) Guests
149] b) Scrabbles

150] b) Direct marketing
151] c) directional advertising
152] d) Way bills
153] c) Bill boards
154] d) Life
155] d) Spectaculars
156] a) Holography

3

PRODUCT MANAGEMENT

1. **Applying 'Euroclean' for satisfying some new and unknown class of needs is an example of ___________.**
   a] need identification
   b] benefit structure analysis
   c] brainstorming
   d] attribute analysis

2. **The ad campaign of MRF:- 'The power of knowledge' is an example of ___________.**
   a] Positioning for user category
   b] Positioning for usage occasion
   c] Positioning on product features
   d] Positioning against another product

3. **The ad campaign of 'Kellog's corn flakes for breakfast' is an example of ___________.**
   a] Positioning on product features
   b] Positioning for user category
   c] Positioning on specific product feature
   d] Positioning on benefit

4. **'Raymond's complete man' campaign is an example of___________.**
   a] Positioning for user category
   b] Positioning for specific usage occasions
   c] Positioning on benefits
   d] Positioning on product features

5. **"Thomas, presents what is missing in other products" is an ad campaign with__________.**
   a] Positioning on benefits
   b] Positioning for user category
   c] Positioning against another product
   d] Positioning for specific usage occasion

6. **The Tata Indica stating- Indian built spacious car is an example of __________.**
   a] product attribute
   b] product benefit
   c] product value
   d] brand image

7. **'Tata Siera owners club' is a concept denoting__________.**
   a] brand association
   b] brand value
   c] brand equity
   d] brand loyalty

8. **Maruti-800 is an example of __________.**
   a] family branding
   b] independent branding
   c] national branding
   d] distributors brand

9. **'D-cold' is the brand name suggesting __________.**
   a] product functioning
   b] specific concept
   c] firms identity
   d] values associated with product

10. **'Nirma' offering a low priced option to the price conscious consumers to gain quick market is an example of__________.**
    a] swimming pricing
    b] penetration pricing
    c] cost plus pricing
    d] discriminatory pricing

11. The ad. that states for every piece of Whisper that you buy RE. 1/- goes for charity is an example of ___________.

a] differentiated pricing
b] perfect profit pricing
c] perceived value pricing
d] cost plus pricing

12. Bring your old T.V. & take a new one at 50% discount is an example of ___________.

a] seasonal discount
b] quantity bulk discount
c] cash discount
d] trade in discount

13. Finding out new products and processes in other areas with an eye towards incorporating them in company's new products is called as ___________.

a] customer analysis
b] active search
c] category analysis
d] competitor analysis

14. Adding few more benefits or features to a product to improve its acceptance is termed as ___________.

a] augmented product
b] product audit
c] product development
d] Product orientation

15. A pricing mechanism for new and highly priced products which bridges the gap between the benefits offered by existing products ___________.

a] churning the market
b] penetration pricing
c] skimming pricing
d] benefit pricing

16. A pricing mechanism where products are priced low to attract wider market segments and to sell in large quantity is ____________.

a] benefit pricing
b] penetration pricing
c] skimming pricing
d] cost based pricing

17. The small market with highly concentrated segmentation of a particular class of buyers result in __________.

a] specialized markets
b] territorial markets
c] segmentated market
d] target market

18. In branding, the extent to which the consumer associates the name of a product to its quality is __________.

a] description value of a name
b] association value
c] memorizational value
d] repurchase value

19. In branding the degree of reliability & name creates _______.

a] purchase value
b] promotional value
c] description value
d] memorization value

20. A brand name, which justifies the expectations raised in the mind of the consumer, is ___________.

a] association value
b] motivational value
c] repurchase value
d] association value

21. While buying a product when buyer considers social values and prevailing cultural forces then, it is an ___________.

a] appeal to senses

b] appeal to a specific buyer class
c] appeal to reason
d] appeal to emotion

22. When a buyer while buying a product compares one brand with another as to know specific benefits or funcitons then it is ___________.
a] appeal to emotion
b] appeal to senses
c] appeal to specific consumer needs
d] appeal to emotions

23. In pure competition, pricing mechanism generally is based on ___________.
a] going rate of the market
b] differentiated pricing
c] target profit pricing
d] perceived value pricing

24. In monopolistic competition the generally accepted pricing policy is ___________.
a] cost plus pricing
b] perceived value pricing
c] going rate pricing
d] differentiated pricing

25. In industries where the pricing is done for various turnkey jobs the suitable mechanism ___________.
a] fixed price policy
b] cost plus
c] bid pricing
d] perceived value pricing

26. When in a market, companies alter prices for different products/customer group, or places it is called ___________.
a] competitive pricing
b] bid pricing
c] target profit pricing
d] discriminatory pricing

27. When the seller offers different prices for different customers for the same products it is ___________.

a] time based discrimination
b] place based discrimination
c] product based discrimination
d] customer based discrimination

28. A stage in the market where it is believed that, there are no competitors is ___________.

a] virtual monopoly
b] monoposny
c] eternal monopoly
d] oligopoly

29. The communication involving body language is popularly termed as ___________.

a] kinesics
b] proxemics
c] paralanguage
d] mass communication

30. Communication system involving arrangement of personal space around us & how we manage it is ___________.

a] chromenics
b] kinesics
c] proxemics
d] para language

31. The manner in which a word is spoken and its impact on the listeners is ___________.

a] kinesics
b] mass communication
c] chromenics
d] paralanguage

32. The speaker who does not make any attempt to supplement the message, rather he is only bothered about the verbal part of the message is ___________.

a] gripper
b] pacer

c] bonvoyager
d] musician

33. A three x three matrix which divides industry attractiveness & business strength in to low medium & high segment is popularly known as ___________.
a] BCG matrix
b] SPI matrix
c] Hober Product matrix
d] McKinsey matrix

34. A two x two product port folio analysis using market growth rate with relative market share is ___________.
a] Arther D Little matrix
b] McKinsey matrix
c] SPI matrix
d] BCG matrix

35. A matrix model based on profit impact market strategy is popularly known as ___________.
a] SPI matrix
b] McKinsey matrix
c] BCG matrix
d] Hobers matrix

36. ______ model suggests that for each business activity with in the corporate portfolio a separate strategy must be developed.
a] BCG matrix
b] McKinsey matrix
c] SPI matrix
d] Hobers product matrix

37. _____ index is based on a thorough environmental assessment influencing the sectoral profitablities.
a] GE matrix
b] PIMs model
c] Hobers model
d] Display matrix

38. The place a product enjoys in a given market is ________.
a] product conception
b] product positioning
c] product status
d] product factor

39. The positioning of a product strongly linked with specific solution, benefit or utility offered by a product is________.
a] usage occasion positioning
b] user category positioning
c] benefit positioning
d] competitive positioning

40. From which of the following segment a marketing research officer can set an unsolicited idea for new product development ___________.
a] sales personnel
b] production department
c] customer service division
d] public

41. The approach of new product development where attempt is made to understand the needs & problems of stakeholders is___________.
a] attribute based identification
b] problem based identification
c] relationship analysis
d] morphological forced connection

42. The approach of new product development where more than two dimensions are combined simultaneously is_____.
a] concept testing
b] relationship analysis
c] morphological analysis
d] attribute based idention

43. A set of all products likes & items that a particular company offers to buyers is ____________.

a] marketing mix
b] product mix
c] augmented product
d] product family

44. Items which are repeatedly used / purchased have a low unit price & little fashion utilities __________.

a] normal commodities
b] shopping goods
c] convenience goods
d] specialty goods

45. Goods purchased after considerable comparison of quality/ price are____________.

a] specialty goods
b] consumer goods
c] shopping goods
d] specialty goods

46. When only one product version is offered for consumer it is ____________.

a] mass marketing
b] target marketing
c] differentiated marketing
d] market segmentation

47. All the products / items that a particular organization makes available to its buyers is termed as __________.

a] product family
b] product mix
c] product class
d] product line

48. The intrinsic worth of the brand in terms of money is____________.

a] brand personality

b] brand image
c] brand equity
d] brand franchise

49. When the buyer is given a product at reduced price at the time of repeat purchase it is termed as ___________.
a] premium package
b] self liquidator
c] coupon pack
d] money off pack

50. In marketing new products includes___________.
a] original products
b] improved products
c] modified products
d] all the above

51. When a product failure results a profit that is less than the company's target rate of return it is ________.
a] partial product failure
b] absolute product failure
c] relative product failure
d] general product failure

52. A ________ product idea is a new product that the company might offer to the market.
a] expected
b] potential
c] possible
d] augmented.

53. A product image is the particular picture that consumers acquire of the product ___________.
a] core features
b] generic features
c] expected features
d] dormant features

54. The product's competition is defined by __________.

a] category concept
b] product idea
c] product image
d] market structure

55. The PLC concept can be used to analyse a __________.

a] product category
b] product form
c] brand
d] none of the above

56. In the life cycle, Emulation stage is the ________ stage.

a] first
b] second
c] third
d] fourth

57. In PLC, the prices tend to be on the higher side in the stage __________.

a] introduction
b] growth
c] maturity
d] decline

58. Company turns on to the product preference advertising in stage of PLC. __________.

a] introduction
b] growth
c] maturity
d] decline

59. When the new product is designed for the middle of the market, the strategy is known as __________.

a] a single niche strategy
b] multiple niche strategy

c] mass market strategy
d] segment market strategy

60. Line-extension trap refers to _________.
a] product line failure risk
b] chance that the brand name will lose its specific meaning
c] innovation is product line
d] product line filling in

61. One of the main incentives for product differentiation in_________.
a] raw material shortage
b] new technology
c] competition
d] economic stagna

62. New market for existing products can be tapped by____.
a] making slight product changes
b] a different marketing approach
c] neither of these
d] both of these

63. During which stage of business cycle organizations tend to expand their marketing programs as they add now products and enter new markets.
a] prosperity
b] recession
c] recovery
d] trough

64. _________ are needed for managing existing product overtime, adding new ones, and dropping failed products
a] strategies
b] policies
c] programmes
d] objectives

65. Of the following the item that is most likely to be a convenience good to most people is __________.

a] a TV set
b] health foods
c] toothpaste
d] hobby supplies

66. Of the following, the item that is most likely to be a shopping good to most people is __________.

a] A TV set
b] health foods
c] toothpaste
d] hobby supplies

67. Of the following classes of industrial goods, top management would be involved in the buying decisions for__________.

a] parts
b] accessory equipment
c] supplies
d] services

68. According to the concept of product life cycle, profits are likely to be highest during the period of ________.

a] introduction
b] growth
c] maturity
d] decline

69. When a product is in the growth stage of its life cycle, a firm should most likely expect __________.

a] a decline in profits
b] an increase in the cost of production
c] competitors entering the market
d] none of the above

70. Creating a different image for product by communicating certain special attributes of a product which were not communicated earlier ___________.

a] Test marketing
b] Repositioning
c] Differentiating
d] High touch positioning

71. Positioning is what a manufacturer does to the __________.

a] product
b] media
c] quality
d] mind of prospect

72. Buyers may find it hard to believe the brand claims made in view of the product's feature, price, or manufacture. This error of positioning is known as __________.

a] confused positioning
b] doubtful positioning
c] under positioning
d] over positioning

73. The items, within a product line that share one of several possible forms of the product, comprises the –

a] product family
b] product class
c] product type
d] need family

74. "Made in Germany" is an example of __________.

a] positioning by price
b] positioning as per quality
c] positioning as per product class
d] positioning as per target market

75. "Environmentally friendly" this is an example of positioning as per ___________.

a] price
b] attribute
c] quality
d] target market

ANSWERS

1] a] need identification
2] c] Pcsitioning on product features
3] d] Positioning on benefit
4] a] Positioning for user category
5] c] Positioning against another product
6] a] prodcut attribute
7] d] brand loyalty
8] c] national branding
9] a] product functioning
10] b] penetration pricing
11] a] differentiated pricing
12] d] trade in discount
13] b] active search
14] a] augmented product
15] c] skimming pricing
16] b] penetration pricing
17] c] segmented market
18] b] association value
19] b] promotional value
20] c] repurchase value
21] d] appeal to emotion
22] d] appeal to emotions
23] a] going rate of the merket
24] d] differentiated pricing
25] c) bid pricing
26] d] discriminatory pricing
27] d] customer based discrimination
28] a] virtual monopoly
29] a] kinesics
30] c] proxemics
31] d] paralanguage
32] a] gripper
33] d] Mckinsey matrix
34] d] BCG matrix
35] a] SPI matrix
36] a] BCG matrix
37] a] GE matrix
38] c) Product status

39] a) usage occasion positioning
40] d] public
41] b) problem based identi
42] c] morphological analysis
43] b] product mix
44] a) normal commodities
45] c) shopping goods
46] a) mass marketing
47] c) product class
48] c) brand equity
49] d) money off pack
50] d) all the above
51] a) partial product failure
52] d) potential
53] a) core features
54] a) category concept
55] b) product form
56] a) first
57] b) growth
58] c) maturity
59] b) multiple niche strategy
60] a) product line failure risk
61] b) new technology
62] a) making slight product change
63] a) prosperity
64] a) strategies
65] b) health foods
66] d) hobby supplies
67] d) services
68] b) growth
69] c) competitors entering the market
70] b) Repositioningo
71] d) mind of prospect
72] b) doubtful positioning
73] b) product class
74] b) positioning as per quality
75] b) attribute

4

MARKET SEGMENTATION

1. **Segmentation where age, gender and occupation are the principal factors to classify consumers is called as____________.**
   a] psychologographic
   b] demographic
   c] behavioural segmentation
   d] geographic

2. **When buyers are divided into various classes on the basis of values, lifestyle or personality it is called as______.**
   a] demographic segmentation
   b] psychographic
   c] behaviour
   d] geographic

3. **The segmentation where variables like ocassional user status and loyalty status are considered as parameters is termed as____________.**
   a] behavior
   b] psychographic
   c] demographic
   d] geographic

4 **Classification of markets according to the benefits the consumers seek from a particular product is ___________.**
   a] benefit segmentation
   b] psychographic
   c] geographic
   d] demographic

5. **A noodle marketer promotes his product as a 'pure vegetarian and nourishing food' is applying the concept of___________.**
   a] benefit segmentation
   b] geographic segmentation
   c] demographic
   d] psychographic

6. **The promotion of 'Thumps Up' as a drink for 'Youth, with vigour' is an example of ___________.**
   a] demographic b] geographic
   c] benefit d] psychographic

7. **"Eve"- a popular cigarette for women consumers is an example of___________.**
   a] benefit segmentation
   b] geographic
   c] demographic
   d] psychographic

8. **'Tastes great and less filling' ad campaign for a beer is an example of ___________.**
   a] behavior segmentation
   b] psychographics
   c] demographic
   d] geographics

9. **'For a self confident and independent man' is an ad slogan based on the concept of ________.**
   a] demographic
   b] psychographic
   c] behavior
   d] benefit segmentation

10. **'Prevent tooth decay – strengthens gums' is an ad slogan depicting ___________.**
    a] benefit segmentation
    b] geographic
    c] behavior
    d] demographic

11. A 'low fat Mc clean burger' is an example of____________.
a] geographic segmentation
b] differentiation positioning
c] head to head positioning
d] psychographic segmentation

12. The way a society organizes its economic activities & physical things for well-being is its____________.
a] material culture b] value system
c] social structure d] economic environment

13. The process of classifying buyers into distinct buyer groups is ____________.
a] positioning
b] targeting
c] segmentation
d] mass marketing

14. Classifying buyer on the basis of their preference for product attribute is____________.
a] preference segmentation
b] product segmentation
c] age segmentation
d] income segmentation

15. The technique of segmenting market on the basis of characteristics of the markets, usage occasion, and relevant market group is____________.
a] spectrum analysis
b] grid analysis
c] target based positioning
d] market analysis

16. Spectrum Analysis is the technique to identify segmentation on the basis of ____________.
a] current product in the same product category
b] new product in the existing product category

c] existing product in the existing market
d] new product in the new market

17. The term psychographic segmentation is coined by_____.
a] W. Schiller
b] D.Ogilivi
c] E.Demby
d] W.Starton

18. When the buyers are classified on the basis of benefits sought from product, usage rate and user status it is called as __________.
a] behavioural segmentation
b] benefit segmentation
c] psychographic segmentation
d] demographic segmentation

19. A distinctive segment of the environment in which the firm does or may want to do business is known as_______.
a] Strategic business area
b] Fly-area
c] Cover area
d] Business environment.

20. To gain the most effect from market segmentation it is important that information relating to buyer be________.
a] accessible
b] measurable
c] capable of analysis
d] all of these.

ANSWERS

1] b] demographic
2] b] psychographic
3] a] behaviour
4] a] benefit segmentation
5] b] geographic segmentation

6] a] demographic
7] c] demographic
8] a] behavior segmentation
9] b] psychographic
10] a] benefit segmentation
11] b] differentiation positioning
12] a] material culture
13] c) segmentaiton
14] a) preference segmentation
15] c) Target based positioning
16] d) new product in the new market
17] c) E. Demby
18] b) benefit segmentation
19] b) Fly area
20] c) capable of analysis

5

CONSUMER BEHAVIOUR

1. The fundamental determinant of a persons wants and behaviour is____________.

a] value system
b] culture
c] ideology
d] philosophy

2. The group that have direct or indirect influence on the persons attitude or behaviour is ____________.

a] reference group
b] primary group
c] membership group
d] external group

3. The group a person hopes/desires to join is____________.

a] secondary group
b] aspirational group
c] opinion group
d] reference group

4. A person in informal group who offers product related advices / information / communication that influences buying behaviour is called ____________.

a] opinion leader
b] group leader
c] idea leader
d] fellow

5. **The set of successful 'take charge' people in a group is called as ____________.**

   a] actualize

   b] achiever

   c] experience

   d] followers.

6. **Successful and work oriented people, who favour prestige products to demonstrate their success ____________.**

   a] users

   b] achievers

   c] makers

   d] strugglers

7. **Conservative and traditional buyers who favour established products are called____________.**

   a] strugglers

   b] makers

   c] believers

   d] strivers

8. **People who are uncertain, insecure, and resource constrained are ____________.**

   a] believers

   b] strivers

   c] makers

   d] strugglers.

9. **The characteristics/traits that influence a persons buying behaviour is____________.**

   a] personality

   b] image

   c] portrait

   d] style

10. **The tendency to twist information into personal meanings and interpret accordingly is ____________.**

    a] selective distortion

    b] selective hearing

    c] selective attention

    d] selective division.

11. **People retain the information that supports their attitude this is called_________.**
    a] selective hearing
    b] selective learning
    c] selective attention
    d] selective retention.

12. **A strong internal stimulus impelling action is__________.**
    a] cues
    b] drive
    c] learning
    d] urge

13. **Minor stimulus that determine when where what and how a person responds is __________.**
    a] discrimination
    b] drive
    c] cues
    d] urge

14. **A person enduring favourable or unfavourable evaluation or emotions towards an object or idea is __________.**
    a] idea
    b] attitude
    c] view
    d] value

15. **The person who first suggests the idea of buying the product or service are _________.**
    a] user
    b] decider
    c] influence
    d] initiator

16. **The person whose views/idea influence the decision is called __________.**
    a] buyer
    b] influencer
    c] initiator
    d] decider

17. The agencies that informative evaluatory data about markets industries or business agencies are____________.

a] intermediaries
b] yellow pages
c] data bank
d] market reports

18. The customers who can value through lowest price.............

a] price oriented customers
b] solution oriented customers
c] routine customers
d] strategic value customers.

19. What usually directs a consumer behavior towards attaining his / her needs ____________.

a] stimuli
b] motive
c] needs
d] desires

20. Conflict resulting from two contradictory beliefs after buying a product is ____________.

a] disconfirmation of expectations
b] post purchase dissonance
c] negative repulse
d] none of the above

21. The stochastic model of consumer behaviour process proposes that ____________.

a] the probability that the consumer will demand same product, in a large no. of cases.
b] the consumer's brand preferences are uncertain
c] there is no relationship between brand loyally & buying behaviour
d] the chances of brand loyally vary from product to product

22. The most important feature of brand loyalty is ___________.

a] it is product specific
b] it is company specific
c] it is segment specific
d] it is low for convenience goods

23. Unplanned purchase is the result of___________.

a] pure impulse
b] inertia
c] passive learning
d] contrast effect

24. A tendency to buy out of whim or action based on a powerful & persistent urge is___________.

a] planned impulse
b] impulse buying
c] suggestion effect
d] reminder effect

25. For a consumer television is a medium of ___________.

a] reminder effect
b] passive learning
c] suggestion effect
d] forced learning

26. When two consumers perceive the identical advertisement product very differentially it is called as___________.

a] selective perception
b] perceptual vigilance
c] perceptual defense
d] perceptual equilibrium

27. The consumer boredom that reduces familiarity and effectiveness of ad is ___________.

a] advertising wear out
b] source loss
c] ad decay
d] ad loss.

28. Activities interest, opinions are called as__________.

a] demographic variables
b] values
c] psychological variables
d] personal variables

29. People seek, confirm, & ascertain a sense of well-being through what they have is their __________.

a] ideal self
b] actual self
c] extended self
d] super ego

30. What controls the individuals most basic needs & urges?

a] super ego
b] id
c] defense mechanism
d] ideal self

31. The process of learning the values of own culture from childhood is___________.

a] sub culture
b] acculturatilsm
c] cultural norm
d] enculturatilsm

32. The power derived from experience & knowledge by the consumer class is___________.

a] expert power
b] reward power
c] referent power
d] coercive power

33. The individuals identification with members in the group provides with,___________.

a] referent power
b] reward power
c] expert power
d] status power

34. Expert power exercises ___________.on the reference group

a] comparative influence
b] normative influence
c] informational influence
d] expert influence

35. Referent power exercise ___________.in the reference group.

a] normative influence
b] comparative influence
c] informational influence
d] reward influence

36. The roles that are related to performing tasks that help the group make final purchasing decision are___________.

a] participative roles
b] instrumental roles
c] expressive roles
d] family roles

37. The roles that facilitate expression of group norms and provide group with social / emotional support are__________.

a] expressive roles
b] assertive roles
c] group roles
d] instrumental roles.

38. The opinion leaders who introduce ideas / information to the group but may not influence it__________.

a] market makers
b] gate keepers
c] surrogate consumers
d] opinion makers.

39. Individuals who are gate-keepers across many categories because of their general expertise are___________.

a] market movers
b] gate keepers
c] opinion maker
d] influential

40. The process of learning culture different from one in which a person was raised is __________.

a] acculturatism

b] trans culturalism

c] incultration

d] decultratizalism

41. People of similar ages who have some same thought and similar experience.

a] life style sharing

b] age cohert

c] value cohert

d] attitude cohert

42. A theory that states that people attribute a cause to their prior behaviour__________.

a] altitude theory

b] attributism theory

c] assimilitism

d] contrast effect theory

43. Identification of a group on consumers based on similarity in needs is called__________.

a] benefit segment

b] blocking effect

c] core segment

d] utility based segmentation

44. A response that is result of influence by primary and secondary stimuli is __________.

a] cognitive response

b] conditioned response

c] comparative influence

d] proximity influence

45. The need to achieve pleasure from a product is__________.

a] id

b] inertia

c] hedonic need

d] safety needs

46. Contrast effect indicates ___________.

a] difference between pleasures expected & actually derived

b] magnified disparity between expectations & experience of consumers

c] disparity between estimated and actual process.

d] none of the above

47. Those standards behavior that govern proper social relations & means of ensuring safety are ___________.

a] cultural norms

b] social norms

c] values

d] deterministic norms

48. A group to which an individual may try to avoid membership ___________.

a] cultural group

b] contrast group

c] dissociative group

d] extinct group

49. The need to achieve pleasure from a product most likely associated with emotions or fantasies derived from consuming a product is___________.

a] habit

b] hedonic need

c] safety needs

d] perceived need

50. A cluster of belief that represents an individuals perception of an object or situation is ___________.

a] schema

b] ritual

c] belief

d] value system

51. When a consumer appears to be brand loyal but is not, still he repurchases it ___________.

a] spurious loyalty

b] dubious loyalty

c] alternative loyalty
d] dummy loyalty

52. One who is determined to buy a product with self driven initiative to fulfill some need ___________.
a] initiator
b] influencer
c] buyer
d] presumers

53. The moment a consumer intends to buy a product he becomes conscious of a particular ad, which he might have earlier ignored is called as___________.
a] selective retention
b] selective distortion
c] selective exposure
d] self learning

54. Consumers loyal to two or three brands are known as___________.
a] hare care loyals
b] split loyals
c] shifting loyals
d] switchers loyals

55. Customers who want easy-to-read manuals hot lines and knowledgeable sales representatives are ___________.
a] novices
b] sophisticates
c] first-time prospects
d] glow suspects

56. Skeptical is the term denoting___________.
a] early majority
b] late majority
c] innovators
d] tradition bound

57. Laggards is the term used for ___________.

a] early majority
b] late majority
c] innovators
d] tradition bound.

58. Venturesome is the term used for ___________.

a] early majority
b] late majority
c] innovators
d] tradition bound

59. Shoppers who view shopping as 'game' and consider getting a bargain as more important are___________.

a] bottom liners
b] opportunities switches
c] deal hunters
d] non strategists

60. The people who set the specification and aspects of buying decisions are known as the ___________.

a] trend setters
b] users
c] influencers
d] decides

61. Consumers perception that many brands are equivalent is ___________.

a] Brand equity
b] Brand ladder
c] Brand battle
d] Brand parity.

62. Credence qualities are the characteristics that the buyer___________.

a] finds hard to evaluate even after consumption
b] cannot evaluate before purchase
c] cannot evaluate after purchase
d] can evaluate any time.

ANSWERS

1] a) value system
2] a) reference group
3] b) aspirational
4] a) opinion leaders
5] c) experiences
6] b) achievers
7] c) believers
8] d) strugglers
9] a) personality
10] a) Selective distortion
11] d) selective retention
12] d) urge
13] a) discrimination
14] b) attitude
15] d) intiator
16] b) influencer
17] b) yellow pages
18] a) price oriented customers
19] a) stimuli
20] a) disconfirmation of expectaions
21] b) the consumers brand preferences are uncertain
22] a) It is product specific
23] b) inertia
24] b) impulse buying
25] b) passive learning
26] a) selective perception
27] c) ad decay
28] c) pyschological variables
29] a) ideal self
30] b) id
31] b) aculturatism
32] b) reward power
33] a) referent power
34] d) Expert influence
35] a) normative influence
36] c) expressive roles
37] c) group roles

38] a) market makers
39] a) market movers
40] b) trans culturalism
41] b) age cohert
42] c) assimilitism
43] d) Utility based segmentation
44] b) conditined response
45] c) hedonic need
46] b) magnified disparity between expectations & experience of consumers
47] b) social norms
48] c) dissociative group
49] b) hedonic need
50] a) schema
51] d) dummy loyalty
52] a) Initiator
53] d) self learning
54] b) split loyals
55] b) sophisticates
56] d) tradition bound
57] b) late majority
58] c) innovators
59] c) deal hunters
60] a) trend, setters
61] d) brand parity
62] d) can evaluate any time.

6

PRICING

1. **The most applicable pricing model for essential commodities is ____________.**
   a] differentiated pricing
   b] tender pricing
   c] affordability pricing
   d] product line pricing

2. **When a firm charges different prices for the same product in different zones of the market is termed __________.**
   a] affordability pricing
   b] tender pricing
   c] differentiated pricing
   d] product line pricing

3. **When the seller takes the maximum price that the customers are willing to pay for the product is ____________.**
   a] penetration pricing
   b] what the traffic can bear
   c] slimming pricing
   d] market based pricing

4. **When the pricing is based on estimated unit cost of the product at normal level of production & sales __________.**
   a] mark up pricing
   b] marginal costing
   c] target rate of return pricing
   d] absorption cost pricing

5. When the selling price of the product is fixed by adding a margin to its cost price is ___________.

a] mark up pricing
b] marginal cost pricing
c] break even pricing
d] penetration pricing

6. A method of quoting approximate price relating to sales volume & value in a foreign market is ___________.

a] probe pricing
b] penetration pricing
c] differential pricing
d] cost pricing

7. A price that may yield marginal surplus over the total cost initially incurred is___________.

a] differential pricing
b] penetration pricing
c] probe pricing
d] cost plus pricing

8. The pricing resorted to by an exporter who has gained a strong foot hold to charge higher price than the normal market price is ___________.

a] probe pricing
b] cost plus pricing
c] slimming pricing
d] competitive pricing

9. When an independent businessman abides by the marketing plan of the marketer & pays him a fee for the use of the brand know how it is called ___________.

a] Agency contract
b] Dealership
c] Sole selling agency
d] Franchisee contract

10. A skimming price policy is usually most suitable for a new product when __________.

a] the seller wants to penetrate a market quickly
b] the product is in its introductory stage and demand is very inelastic
c] the product is in its maturity stage and demand is very inelastic
d] demand is elastic

11. A pricing policy of setting up definite price lines or zones and selling goods only in those ranges or zones is known as __________.

a] promotional pricing
b] premium pricing
c] odd pricing
d] price lining

12. One problem involved in price lining is that __________.

a] it complicates the buying function
b] it complicates the pricing function
c] it cannot be used with odd pricing
d] cost-plus pricing must be used with it.

13. The element in the marketing mix that is most subject to legal control is __________.

a] product
b] distribution
c] price
d] promotion

14. Price is a particular challenge for sellers of __________.

a] highly differentiated products
b] products associated with a particular brand name
c] products not associated with a particular brand name
d] highly standardized items.

15. If a seller can differentiate his brand in the buyer's mind the seller may be able to __________.

a] initiate new product lines

b] raise prices somewhat higher than those of competing sellers
c] decrease their costs
d] raise the prices of competing brands

16. A trade discount is a reduction from the list price that a manufacturer gives to ___________.

a] the ultimate consumer
b] other manufacturers
c] wholesalers and retailers
d] employees of the firm.

17. A seller who decides to "skim the cream" ___________.

a] charges the lowest possible price
b] charges the highest possible price
c] charges a moderate price
d] lets the customer determine a reasonable price.

ANSWERS

1] c] affordable pricing
2] c] differentiated pricing
3] b] what the traffic can bear
4] d] absorption cost pricing
5] a] mark up price
6] a] probe pricing
7] b] penetration pricing
8] c] slimming pricing
9] d) Franchisee contract
10] b) the product is in its introductory stage and demand is very inelastic
11] d) price lining
12] c) it cannto be used with odd pricing
13] c) price
14] b) products associated with a particular brand name.
15] b) rise prices some what higher than those of competing sellers.
16] c) wholesellers and retailers
17] d) charges the highest possible price

7

MARKET SELECTION

1. **The GDP of the country & per capita GDP is a good indicator for MNC to decide___________.**
   a] market potential
   b] level of competition
   c] purchasing power
   d] socio-cultural environment

2. **For a MNC, the size of product-market in terms of unit size & sales volume helps to decide___________.**
   a] competitor analysis
   b] product market dimension
   c] structural aspects of product market
   d] strategic option

3. **Proactive motivations for exporting are__________.**
   a] opportunities available in host countries
   b] indirect export opportunities
   c] high risk export practices
   d] direct export opportunities

4. **When a company outsource its parts of or entire production & concentrate on marketing operation it is called as____.**
   a] management contract
   b] turkey project
   c] contract manufacturing
   d] franchising agreement

5. When an independent organization operates the business under the name of another company to trade & produce and acquires advantage of support system it is called as____________.

a] licensing b] export intermediary
c] franchisee d] contract marketing

6. A contract where a firm agrees to fully design & turn the project over to the purchaser when it is ready for operation for a remuneration it is___________.

a] management contract
b] franchisee
c] licencing
d] turnkey project

7. The strategy to start with a virgin green site & then building on it is called as___________.

a] FDI strategy
b] Green field strategy
c] Licensing
d] Franchising

8. A cooperative & collaborative approach to achieve the larger goals is____________.

a] green field strategy
b] competitive coalitions
c] joint venture
d] strategic alliance

9. Two or more firms join together to create a new business entity that is legally separate and distinct from its parents____________.

a] strategic alliance
b] joint venture
c] competitive coalition
d] management contract

10. __________ is an alliance of two or more companies joining together to reduce financial risk associated with project.

a] Financial alliance

b] Production alliance

c] R & D alliance

d] Marketing alliance

11. Interdependency & integration of individual countries of the world is ___________.

a] Economic union

b] Trade blocks

c] World economy

d] Globalization

12. The year of establishment of GATT is___________.

a] 1947 b] 1950

c] 1944 d] 1942

13. Gatt came into existence at a trade conference held at___________.

a] Brusells

b] Geneva

c] Brettonwoods

d] Chicago

14. GATT stands for ___________.

a] General Agreement on Trade & Tarrifs

b] General Agreement on Trade & Transaction

c] General Agreement on Trade Treaty

d] General Agreement on Technical Treaty

15. GATT is a ___________.

a] competent trade authority

b] a uniform trade rule clause

c] set of rules and multilateral agreement

d] a union of European countries

16. WTO is a/an ___________.

a] multilateral trade agreement

b] permanent institution

c] multinational bank

d] agency of UNO

17. The Final Draft of WTO was signed in the year

a] 1992

b] 1994

c] 1991

d] 1990

18. The ministerial meet for finalization of WTO agreement was held at ___________.

a] Marrakesh

b] Uruguay

c] Singapore

d] Doha

19. WTO was established in the year ___________.

a] 1997

b] 1996

c] 1994

d] 1995

20. TRIP stands for ___________.

a] Trade Related Interested Party

b] Trade Related Intellectual Party

c] Trade relational Interest & Parity

d] Trade Related Intellectual Property

21. MFN Stands for

a] Mutually Favorable Nation

b] Most Favored Nation

c] Most Famous Nation

d] Minimum Favorable Nation

22. GATS stands for___________.

a] General Agreement on Trade in Services

b] General Agreement on Tariff Size

c] General Agreement on Technical Sector

d] General Agreement on Tertiary Sector

23. Design & Patents are included in which part of GATT

a] TRIM

b] TRIP

c] GATS

d] MFN

24. Selling the product at below the ongoing market price is___________.

a] Protective measure

b] MAI

c] Dumping

d] Trade facilitation

25. When a monopolist sells a product in foreign market at low price to reduce competition it is___________.

a] Persistent Dumping

b] Predatory Dumping

c] Intermittent Dumping

d] Restricted Dumping

26. When an importing country bans the import of a particular goods or all the goods from a particular country it is termed as________.

a] voluntary export restraints

b] tariff duty

c] import quota

d] import embargo

27. MAI stands for ___________.

a] Multilateral Agreement on Investment

b] Multinational Agency for Investment

c] Multiple Agreements on Investment

d] Mutual Agreement on Investment

28. Tax imposed on imports is ___________.

a] Levy

b] Duty

c] Octroi

d] Tariff

29. The tariff levied in the proportion of value of imported goods is ___________.

a] Specific tariff

b] Ad valorem

c] Subsidies

d] Special tariff

30. A direct restriction on the commodity of goods which are imported into a country is ___________.

a] import quota

b] voluntary export restraints

c] embargoes

d] boycott

31. FCN treaty means __________.

a] Free Commodity Navigation

b] Friendship Commerce Navigation

c] Freight Cartage & Negotiation

d] Freight Cargo Navigation

32. G7 Countries include __________.

a] Seventy seven developing country as a block

b] Seventy seven developed country as a block

c] Seventy seven undeveloped country as a block

d] Seventy seven backward economies

33. If a group of countries agree to abolish all trade restrictions & barriers then it is called as __________.

a] Economic union

b] MFN

c] Common market

d] Free trade area

34. When the member countries of a union agree to adopt uniform commercial policy of barriers with regard to trade with non member countries it is called __________.

a] Economic union

b] Common market

c] Customs union

d] Free trade area

35. Extended marketing segmentation into more finite components is __________.

a] micro segmentation

b] micro marketing

c] in depth analysis

d] micro analysis

36. The term used interchangeably for 'Target market' is____________.

a] potential market

b] served market

c] available market

d] penetrated market

37. In estimating total market potential, the total population referred as to be____________.

a] suspect pool

b] prospect pool

c] hot-prospect pool

d] average pool

38. The act of establishing and communicating the product key distinctive benefits in the market is referred as________.

a] market segmentation

b] market targeting

c] market positioning

d] market featuring

39. When the consumer preferences are scattered throughout the space it is termed as____________.

a] heterogeneous preferences

b] diffused preferences

c] clustered preferences

d] junk preferences

ANSWERS

1] c) Purchasing power

2] d) strategic option

3] a) Opportunities available in host countries

4] d) Franchising agreement

5] a) licensing

6] d) turnkey project

7] b) Green field strategy
8] c) joint venture
9] d) management contract
10] a) financial alliance
11] b) Trade blocks
12] a) 1947
13] c) Brettonwoods
14] a) General Agreement on Trade & Tarriffs
15] c) set of rules and multilateral agreement
16] b) A permanent instituton
17] a) 1992
18] b) uruguay
19] c) 1994
20] d) Trade Related Intellectual Property
21] b) Most Favoured Nation
22] a) General Agreement on Trade in Services
23] b) TRIP
24] a) Protective measures
25] b) Predatory Dumping
26] d) import embargo
27] a) Multilateral Agreement on Investiment
28] d) Tariff
29] b) Ad valourem
30] a) Import quota
31] a) Free Commodity Navigation
32] a) Seventy seven developing country as a block
33] a) Economic union
34] c) Customs union
35] c) in depth analysis
36] a) potential market
37] c) hot prospect pool
38] c) market positioning
39] a) heterogeneous preferences

8

SALES PROMOTION

1. Increasing sales volume or exceeding quota in an incentive programme is called as ____________.

a] Add on award

b] Premium quota

c] Incentive quota

d] Extra performance goal

2. A display containing different sizes, colour & types of items, etc. is called ____________.

a] Multiple Display

b] Variety Display

c] Assortment Display

d] Classified Display

3. The on pack premium offered on a product is called as____________.

a] Branded Premium

b] Ordinary Premium

c] Full pack Premium

d] Special Premium

4. A sales offer providing additional quantity of the product free, on purchase of regular quantity at regular price is called____________.

a] patronage offer
b] gift
c] bonus pack
d] special Offer

5. A promotional offer to refund part of the purchase price of a product to consumers who send proof of purchase to the marketer____________.

a] tear off coupon
b] buy back
c] bonus pack
d] cash refund offer

6. ____________ is an attitude change theory that postulates consumers act to relieve discomfort that occurs as a result of conflicting information.

a] Classical conditioning
b] Cognitive learning
c] Cognitive dissonance
d] Behavioral learning

7. A form of learning that involves thought & conscious awareness is called ____________.

a] Conditional learning
b] Cognitive learning
c] Complex learning
d] Passive learning

8. **Sales promotion directed at the ultimate uses of the product is ___________.**

   a] consumer sales promotion

   b] discount

   c] coupon plan

   d] pop promotion

9. **A premium offered to a retailer for specified purchases_____.**

   a] direct premium

   b] dealer loader

   c] display loader

   d] retailer premium

10. **A dealer incentive which is part of PoP is termed as_________.**

    a] door opener premium

    b] display loader

    c] dealer premium

    d] dealer loader

11. **A free premium to build traffic is called ___________.**

    a] hostess gift

    b] in pack premium

    c] give away

    d] lottery

12. **Additional sales produced by the sales promotion _________.**

    a] impulse sales

    b] incremental sales

    c] extra sales

    d] coupon sales

13. A decision making process that requires search for information and evaluation of alternatives ___________.

a] complex decision making

b] decision making

c] critical decision making

d] system oriented decision making

14. The realization by the consumers that there is a difference between 'What is?' & 'What should be?' is ________.

a] cognitive dissonance

b] cognitive learning

c] need recognition

d] self perception

15. A negative or unpleasant outcome that discourages repetition of specified behavior ___________.

a] negative reinforcement

b] negative recognition

c] negative learning

d] negative dissonance

16. Display or demonstration that takes place at the point of sale is called ___________.

a] Off pack display

b] POP display

c] Motion display

d] Window display

17. A price reduction from regular price is ___________.

a] patronage award

b] price discount

c] special discount

d] rebate

18. A certain amount of money given back by the marketer when a customer submit proof of purchase is called______.

a] Prize b] Discount

c] Rebate d] Premium

19. An incentive to the consumer for the regular use of a certain product.

a] Prize

b] Patronage Reward

c] Rebate

d] Discount

20. An extra monetary incentive given to sales people for performing specified task.

a] patronage reward

b] push money

c] cash incentive

d] reward

21. A premium offered to a customers at a price which makes the scheme entirely consumer supported.

a] Bonus

b] Reward

c] Incentive

d] Self liquidator

22. Push money paid to the sales people to promote a particular product.

a] Reward

b] Bonus

c] Incentive

d] Spiff

23. __________ is a market segment that can be best served from the competitive point of view.

a] Target market

b] Benefit segment

c] Specialized market

d] Classified market

24. A cooperative promotion effort featuring two or more products __________.

a] spiffs

b] trade promotion

c] twin promotion

d] tie in promotion

25. A firm sponsoring charity or a cause that it then links to its name is __________.

a] social marketing

b] cause related marketing

c] consumer case marketing

d] green marketing.

26. The compensation system that maximizes the sales manager's control over the salesperson's activity is __________.

a] salary

b] commission

c] salary plus commission

d] expenses

27. The compensation system that maximizes incentive is__________.

a] salary

b] commission

c] salary plus commission

d] expenses.

28. In formulized selling, the salesperson should first formulate a definite sales strategy or plan during which stage?

a] pre approach
b] approach
c] prospecting
d] contact.

29. Sellers offer quantity discount to induce customers to buy____________.

a] more frequently
b] in larger amount
c] one particular
d] a number of different brand.

30. If a retailer is offered a 30% discount from the wholesaler, the discount is termed ____________.

a] a cash discount
b] a trade discount
c] a sales discount
d] none of the above.

31. Under achiever is a person who ____________.

a] performs less due to poor motivation
b] performs less due to low morale
c] a person who refuses to work
d] achieves less than he is capable of for want of challenging job.

32. A premium given to a retailer by a manufacturer for buying a certain quantity of product is____________.

a] push money
b] buying allowance
c] kinctography
d] spectaculars.

33. Sales promotion cannot___________.

a] obtain trial of a new product

b] increase consumption of a product

c] neutralize competitive promotions

d] build brand loyalty.

34. Sales promotion can___________.

a] build brand loyalty

b] establish a purchasing pattern by persuading triers to rebuy

c] reverse a declining sales trend

d] convert rejection of an inferior product into acceptance.

35. A type of public relations advertising that deals with public welfare issues and is typically run free of charge is referred as___________.

a] Publicity

b] Advocacy advertising

c] Green marketing

d] Public service announcements.

36. Business advertising is used primarily to___________.

a] create instant market for the product

b] to support distribution of the product

c] to support and assist the selling function

d] to create new users and markets.

37. To receive coupon money retailers must send the manufacturer the pages from a news paper on which an ad appears is technically termed as___________.

a] Cutting

b] Tearsheet

c] Ad spot

d] Location spot

ANSWERS

1] b) premum quota
2] a] multiple display
3] d] special premum
4] b] Gift
5] a) Tear off coupons
6] c] Cognitive dissonance
7] a) conditional learning
8] d) pop promotion
9] d] retailer premium
10] b] display loader
11] c] give away
12] b] incremental sales
13] c] critical decision making
14] c] need recognition
15] a] negative reinforcement
16] b] POP display
17] b] price discount
18] c] rebate
19] b) patronage reward
20] b] push money
21] d) Self liquidator
22] d] spiff
23] c) Specialised market
24] d] tie in promotion
25] b) cause related marketing
26] b) commission
27] c) Salary plus commission
28] a) Preapproach
29] b) In larger amount
30] c) A sales discount
31] d) achieves less than he is capable of for want of challenging job.
32] d) spectaculess
33] c) Neutralize competitive promotions
34] c) reverse a delining sales trend.
35] b) Advocacy advertising
36] c) To support and assist the selling funciton
37] b) Tearsheet

9

MARKETING RESEARCH

1. **When the observers watch specifically what they are told to study in a precisely formulated problem it is ________.**

   a] laboratory setting observation

   b] disguised observation

   c] structured observation

   d] direct observation

2. **A list of questions framed to set the facts opinion and views is ________.**

   a] structured observation

   b] interview schedule

   c] data sheet

   d] questionnaire

3. **The questions with only two possible answers are________.**

   a] Open ended   b] Multiple choice

   c] Unstructured   d] Dichotomous

4. **Individuals mental processors that determine both the actual/potential response of each person is__________.**

   a] value   b] attitude

   c] belief   d] moves

5. **A scale in which number serve as labels to identify persons objects or event is __________.**

a] rational scale b] ordinal scale

c] nominal scale d] interval scale

6. **A market research survey undertaken to evaluate the perception about a particular brand by people is _________.**

a] image evaluation

b] public opinion survey

c] copy testing

d] test marketing

7. **A market research undertaken to evaluate leading companies or brands are viewed in the minds of consumers concerning key product or image attributes is___________.**

a] market share analysis

b] positioning studies

c] location studies

d] media measurement

8. **Conjoint analysis is used ___________.**

a] to measure sales performance

b] to measure consumer preference for alternate product ideas & product attributes

c] to measure product performance

d] to measure ad. Effectiveness

9. **Multi Dimensional scaling deals with __________.**

a] utility of a particular ad-campaign

b] graphically portray consumer evaluation of products

c] utility of retail audit

d] effectivity of ad. Panels.

10 Consumer panels are used for measuring ____________.

a] product performance analysis

b] effectivity of POP

c] success of a ad. campaign

d] utility of a market survey.

11. Sampling bias indicates____________.

a] it is the bias that sets into the sampling procedure unconsciously

b] failure to collect right sample

c] errors due to small size of sample

d] deficiencies in the nature of sample

12. Sampling error means__________.

a] poor quality of sample

b] inadequacy of sample

c] improper technique of sample selection

d] the basic defect in sampling method

13. A panel research is associated with __________.

a] using the same sample over & over again for collection of information

b] continuous survey of market

c] survey by experts

d] variation in market structure.

14. Judgement sampling is a __________.

a] selection of a permanent sample

b] systematically defined sample

c] deliberate choice of a sample based on judgement

d] selection of a quota sample on predetermined parameters

15 **Consumer care panel is a way to understand ___________.**

a] quality of services offered
b] risks offered in services
c] competition in the services marketing
d] understanding consumer expectations

16. **Credit rating of dealers is a concept useful to a marketer____.**

a] to ascertain cost of distribution
b] to improve distribution not work
c] to fix different credit limit
d] to control losses due to poor sales

17. **MODE in the field of marketing research stands for_________.**

a] Multinational Organizational Design Encore
b] Market Oriented Data Enterprise
c] Marketing Operations Design & Enquiry Services
d] Marketing Operations & Delivery Enclave

18. **MRAS stands for ___________.**

a] Marketing Research and Analytical Services
b] Marketing Research Agency for Services
c] Marketing Research Advisory Services
d] Marketing of Regional & Area Services

19. **The qualitative marketing research concentrates on________.**

a] quantitative aspects of analysis
b] provides insights on marketing problem
c] involves a specific research enquiry
d] summarises data non numerically

20. **Multi-dimensional scaling is used for ___________.**

a] a graphical portrait of consumers evaluation of products

b] a market analysis for new product
c] sales analysis of new products
d] market share analysis of a company

21. The main purpose of advertising audience panel is________.

a] to know about the brand preferences
b] to evaluate the product utility
c] to gather valuable information for media planning
d] to collect information about market structure in a territory

22. Retail Audit helps to know

a] sales analysis of a product
b] dealers & retailers relationship
c] effectivity of promotional campaigns for retailers
d] purchasing pattern of retailers

23. In panel research the researcher

a] stresses on qualitative aspects of data
b] uses the same sample over and over again for collecting the data
c] emphasis on appointing experts to evaluate the performance
d] constitutes the variety of techniques to improve the quality of data.

24. Response error is the example of___________.

a] semantic error
b] non sampling error
c] sampling error
d] sampling bias

25. Too small a sample results in___________.

a] sampling error

b] sampling bias

c] processing error

d] coding errors

26. A deliberate choice of sampling based on population members is termed as____________.

a] Random sampling

b] Panel sampling

c] Sampling bias

d] Judgement sampling

27. When the sampling stratification is based on criteria of location it is called as ____________.

a] Systematic sampling

b] Quota sampling

c] Panel sampling

d] Area sampling

28. Systematic sampling involves____________.

a] deciding a particular method of sample selections

b] involves selecting every nth unit from the population

c] selection on criteria of location

d] sample units are selected at random

29. A statement that explain the true characteristics of entire population is called as____________.

a] statistic

b] sample

c] parameter

d] yardstick

30. The degree of closeness between a statistic & a parameter is____________.

a] bias
b] precision
c] sample
d] variable

31. The probability of a parameter lying within the range of error is____________.

a] sampling error
b] sampling bias
c] confidence limit
d] precision

32. A five point scale to assess degree of respondents agreement is____________.

a] Ordinal scale
b] Likert scale
c] Multidimensional scaling
d] Semantic differential

33. Semantic differential concept is coined by____________.

a] Likert
b] Pearson
c] Mahalnobis
d] Osgood

34. Questionnaire is the tool to collect ____________.

a] statistical data
b] opinions & views
c] facts based data
d] behaviour related data

35. Tell-me business is a __________.

a] kind of publication

b] industrial buying guide

c] telephone directory

d] data that can be hired through telephone

36. The heart of all marketing research activities is__________.

a] statistics

b] customer data base

c] research instruments

d] data collection

37. The life style, buying habits & requirements of customers is called as__________.

a] market enquiry

b] customer data base

c] customer surveys

d] consumer survey

38. The automated analysis of large data sets stored in data ware house with a view to finding pattern earlier undiscovered is__________.

a] data warehousing

b] marketing intelligence

c] customer data base

d] data mining

39. Activity quota indicates__________.

a] no. of units to be sold

b] no. of territories to be visited

c] no. of sales calls to be made

d] no. of retailers to be visited

40. A sales territory indicates____________.

a] the ideal sales to be made by sales person

b] sales effectiveness

c] the work load to be assigned to a sales person

d] geographical grouping of customers

41. TRP stands for ____________.

a] Thematic rating point

b] Television rating point

c] Telemeter rating point

d] Tele Brand rating point

42. The measure of viewership of a television programme is called____________.

a] DART   b] TRP

c] ART   d] AAT

43. DAGMAR concept is given by____________.

a] Russel Colley

b] Elton Mayo

c] Theodor Levitt

d] John D.C. Little

44. When Experts in the specific field are asked to evaluate and judge a situation it is called ____________.

a] Extensive opinion

b] Experts opinion

c] Delphi method

d] Range forecast method

45. The model that explains how the buying behaviour of a consumer is influenced by firms activities is called as____________.

a] Psychological model

b] Nicosia model

c] Learning model

d] Economic model

46. A small group of people who are invited to spend a few hours with a skilful moderator to discuss a product is___________.

a] group dynamics

b] group inquiry

c] focus group

d] observational research.

47. The data that can be acquired by scanning data catalogues, to understand purchasing behaviour is ___________.

a] survey research

b] experimental research

c] behavioural research

d] focused research.

48. The purpose of this research is to capture cause and effect relationship____________.

a] experimental research

b] behavioural research

c] survey research

d] mechanical research

49. A scale connecting two bipolar words to indicate opinion of the respondent is called ___________.

a] Likert scale

b] psychological scale.

c] rating scale.

d] importance scale

50. A statement with which respondents shows the amount of agreement/disagreement___________.

a] importance scale

b] Likert scale

c] psychological scale

d] rating scale.

51. The sample in which every member of the population has equal chance of selection____________.

a] simple random sample
b] cluster sample
c] judgment & sample
d] quota sample

52. The population under this sampling plan is divided into mutually exclusive group____________.

a] simple random sample
b] quota sample.
c] judgement sample.
d] stratified random

53. When the researcher selects the most accessible population member it is called____________.

a] cluster sample
b] quota sample
c] convenience sample
d] judgement sample

54. A sampling technique where the researcher selects population members who are good prospects for accurate information is called____________.

a] judgement sample
b] quota sample
c] random sample
d] convenience sample

55. In .... method, the researcher adopts principles of observation, formulation of hypothesis and testing the resiable.

a] skepticism
b] creativity

c] scientific

d] experimental research

56. This kind of marketing research can harm or annoy customer, but may benefit the company__________.

a] Ethical marketing

b] Healthy skepticism

c] Scientific method

d] Intended research

57. A statistical technique for estimating a 'best fitting' equation showing show the value of a dependent variable varies with no. of independent variable is __________.

a] correlation analysis

b] discriminate analysis

c] factor analysis

d] multiple regression analysis

58. A statistical technique whereby respondents' ranked preferences for different offers are analysed to evaluate utilityis called __________.

a] conjoint analysis

b] cluster analysis

c] factor analysis

d] correlation

59. A statistical technique for separating into specified number of mutually exclusive groups to form relatively homogenous group is__________.

a] factor analysis

b] multiple correlation

c] regression

d] cluster analysis.

60. **The model indicating probability of moving from a current state to any future state is ....**

a] market process model

b] queuing model.

c] new product pretest model

d] product pretest model.

61. **The model which shows waiting time and a queue length that can be expected in a system ____________.**

a] queuing model

b] market model

c] sales response model

d] mechanical model.

62. **The technique that allows finding the maximum or minimum value along a well behaved function is ________.**

a] game theory

b] statically decision theory

c] heuristics

d] calculus

63. **The process of measuring consumer preferences for alternative products is ___________.**

a] conjoint analysis

b] morphological analysis

c] marketing mapping

d] business analysis

64. **To identify a business opportunity or define a research problem in a precise manner one has to undertake________.**

a] exploratory research

b] causal research

c] descriptive research

d] analytical research

65. To understand the likely response of consumers to imported readymade garments in a semi urban area in India the research agency should undertake

a] market research

b] exploratory research

c] analytical research

d] causal research

66. A commercial bank wants to know the utility of multipurpose credit card it has launched in last summer. What kind of research it should undertake?

a] Market research

b] Exploratory research

c] Descriptive research

d] Export factor research

67. A market research agency wants to know the utility & application of a particular research instrument that it wants to use for collection of demographic data. What kind of data it should use?

a] Primary data

b] Secondary data

c] Market data

d] Competitive data

68. In order to access the market acceptance for a newly introduced drinking chocolate the company should go for____________.

a] test marketing

b] experimentation

c] pilot study

d] consumer panel research

69. What aspect of a consumer can be studied with the help of a statement "I likc the taste of health food" with options agree, disagree strongly disagree and strongly 'agree?

a] Life style data b] Attitude

c] Socio-economic data d] Intentions

70. The information regarding stores shopped by the consumers indicates ___________.

a] behavioral aspects

b] state of being

c] state of mind

d] volume of sale

71. What technique a researcher interested in controlling all activities of completing a market survey in Mumbai market in a specified firm span should apply for completion of research process?

a] Flow chart

b] Check list

c] PERT

d] Gnatt chart

72. A firm that has introduced eight new detergents in last 3 years should look for__________.

a] subjective estimate

b] empirical evidence

c] deductive method

d] probability technique

73. In order to estimate sequence of all actions-events combination regarding launching of a new detergent a company should use____________.

a] probability technique

b] action projection

c] decision tree approach

d] baysian analysis

74. A soft drink company is interested in knowing how the units responds to price changes then it should consider

a] product related details

b] company policies

c] sales analysis

d] environmental conditions

75. In a business where sales are on decline, the management may undertake a quick study of past sales figures to identify the reasons. This study is called as____________.

a] descriptive study

b] exporatory study

c] cross sectional study

d] longitudinal study

76. To collect information about overall growth of steel industry one should use____________.

a] secondary data

b] primary data

c] metric data

d] external data

77. In order to know the movement of goods from the retail stores a researcher should adopt ____________.

a] observation method

b] interview

c] laboratory experimentation

d] scaling technique

78. In order to assess the impact of messages given by an advertisement the researcher should use ____________.

a] observation method

b] attitudinal study

c] secondary data

d] interview technique

79. When the researcher wants to rank two or more households according to their annual income he should use ___________.

a] interval scales

b] ratio scales

c] ordinal scales

d] nominal scales

80. In the research process a telephone directory can help to develop a ___________.

a] universe

b] sample

c] sampling frame

d] method of sampling

81. If a detergent seller faces a problem of large volumes of sales & low profitability then he should conduct ___________.

a] sales analysis by consumers

b] sales analysis by product

c] sales analysis by territory

d] sales analysis by size of order

82. In order to assess and collect the feedback related to the image of a company, it should undertake___________.

a] public opinion survey

b] iracking study

c] image evaluation study

d] ad. penetration study

83. The statement " people in Gujrat favor a particular flavour of product feature more than the people in Maharashtra" is an example of___________.

a] hypothesis

b] research objective

c] research problem

d] research purpose

84. A research inqu y related with analyzing fall in sales is an example of ___________.

a] descriptive research

b] exploratary research

c] causal research

d] test marketing

85. The data that deals with personality traits, intervals and values of people collected for a specific research enquiry. So as to popularize a soft drink is an example of___________.

a] secondary data

b] classified data

c] primary data

d] experimentation data

86. When there is a general direction to the association between the two variable it is called as___________.

a] nonmontonic association

b] montonic association

c] curvilinear

d] linear

87. The scale that posses the power of determination of equality of differences is___________.

a] interval scale

b] ordinal scale

c] nominal scale

d] ratio scale

88. The measure of reliability of test is ___________.

a] giving the same result under ideal condition

b] variations to a limited extent

c] no change in norms of comparisons

d] represents the true differences in characteristics under study

89. **The ability of the researcher to guess the future performance from the knowledge of the attitude score is___________.**
 a] concurrent validation
 b] predictive validity
 c] construct validity
 d] content validity

90. **The attitude scale on one variable can be used to estimate scores of another variable is termed as ___________.**
 a] predictive validity
 b] concurrent validity
 c] construct validity
 d] content validity

91. **The scale that requires the respondent to pick two objects of set with regard to an attribute of interest is called as___________.**
 a] Thurstone scale
 b] summated rating
 c] scalogram analysis
 d] paired comparison scale

92. **The scaling technique which believes that ordering of certain stimuli is possible is___________.**
 a] Likert scale
 b] scalogram
 c] summated rating scale
 d] Thurstone rating scale
 e] paired comparison

93. **When the units are different at different stages of sampling it is called as___________.**
 a] multiple sampling
 b] frame
 c] biased sample

d] random sampling

94. A sampling technique which gives every unit of population known and non zero probability of being selected is________.

a] random sampling

b] systematic sampling

c] stratified random sampling

d] cluster sampling

95. Quasi random sampling involves____________.

a] calculating sampling fraction

b] selection of independent sample

c] population divided into mutually exclusive strata

d] equal chances of selection for each unit.

96. The sampling technique in which two or more sub samples are drawn and processed completely independent of each other is____________.

a) multi phased sampling

b) sequential sampling

c) quota sampling

d) replicated sampling

97. A sample from which repeated sub samples can be taken as and when required from the same area of population____________.

a] master sample

b] judgement sample

c] quota sample

d] panel sample

98. The sample in which the same unit or element are measured on subsequent occasions are____________.

a]convenience sample

b] panel samples

c] master samples

d] quota samples

99. A proposition which a researcher wants to verify is______.

a] assumption

b] theory

c] theorem

d] hypothesis

100. The error that determines the sensitivity or precision of the experimental procedure is___________.

a] probability error

b] sampling error

c] experimental error

d] technical error

101. The analysis of actual sales result is termed as___________.

a] sales analysis

b] performance analysis

c] market analysis

d] demand analysis

102. The maximum demand response possible for a given group of customers in a defined geographical area is______.

a] sales analysis

b] demand analysis

c] market potential

d] business forecast

103. When the sales forecast is done by the executives instead of sales force it is___________.

a] field sales force

b] users expectations

c] delphi method

d] jury of executives

104. The forecasting method based on experts opinion and regular evaluation of their opinion is called_________.

a] delphi method

b] jury of executives

c] field sales method

d] qualitative method

105. The model concerned with use of statistical and mathematical techniques to verify a hypothesis is________.

a] input output analysis

b] econometric model

c] regression model

d] basic model

106. The technique in which the participants give their view points and as more and more facts are gradually interjected the decision becomes more specific is termed as_________.

a] brain storming

b] synetics

c] problem analysis

d] morphological analysis

107. A technique of concept testing where a respondent evaluates a single item in isolation from other alternatives is________.

a] focus group interview

b] paired comparison

c] monadic test

d] conjoint analysis

108. A controlled experiment in the market place aimed at profit or sales consequences is___________.

a] test marketing

b] market research

c] business analysis

d] business model building

109. A projective technique in which the respondent is given a list of words at a time and asked to mention the first word that comes to his mind is___________.

a] thematic appreciation test

b] word association test

c] recall test

d] recognition test

110. A projective technique consisting of one or more copy righted pictures depicting a situation which the respondent is asked to describe___________.

a] word association test

b] thematic appreciation test

c] two tailed test

d] concept testing

111. A measure used to compare two or more sampling plans is__________.

a] sampling

b] comparative sampling

c] statistical efficiency

d] test related reliability

112. A statistics used in ordinal data to measure the extent of relationship between two variables is__________.

a] Spearman's rank correlation method

b] Soloman's four group design

c] Multidimensional scaling

d] Longitudinal study

113. A judgemental sample in which respondents selected earlier are asked to identify other sample members_______.

a] solomons for group design

b] snow ball design

c] salogram analysis

d] research design.

114. A measure of the effect of seasonal variation is __________.

a] seasonal index

b] rating scale

c] price index

d] significance index

115. A complete list of elements comprising the population from which a sample is to be selected____________.

a] sample statistics

b] sampling unit

c] sampling fraction

d] sampling frame

116. The frequently drawn distribution of all possible samples of a certain size drawn from a particular population is____________.

a] response rate

b] sampling distribution

c] sampling frame

d] sampling units

117. The proccdure in advertising used to ascertain respondents ability to recall aided or unaided is __________.

a] recall test

b] response test

c] simulated test

d] TA test.

118. The tendency on the part of the respondents to prefer responses on account of their position in the list that contains all responses_____________.

a] preferred bias

b] order bias

c] status bias

d] position bias

119. The test in which the respondents are asked t o go through the portfolio containing the advertisements & then asked to recall them is ____________.

a] TAT
b] WAT
c] portfolio test
d] recall test

120. A scale of measurement in which objects or alternatives are arranged in a certain order is ____________.

a] rating scale
b] Likert scale
c] original scale
d] monadic test

121. _________ is a fixed sample of respondents who are interviewed on different variables over a period of time.

a] panel study
b] omnibus panel
c] universal panel
d] consumer panel

122. A statement about the status quo that will prevail on account of random error in the research process is an example of_____________.

a] null hypothesis
b] general hypothesis
c] likert hypothesis
d] none of these

123. An error on account of refusal to supply information by the respondents

a] non sampling error
b] non parametric error
c] non response error
d] non probability sampling

124. **A scale in which numbers are used only to identify or catagorise objects or events without ordcring the categories____________.**

a] original scale
b] nominal scale
c] likert scale
d] rating scale

125. **A problem arising in multiple regression analysis when two or more independent variables are correlated with each other is____________.**

a] multi vaniate analysis
b] multi phase samplings
c] multi collinearity
d] multiple regression

126. **An experimental error that occurs when some respondents withdraw from an experiment before its completion is____________.**

a] sampling error
b] probability error
c] experimental error
c] mortality effect

127. **An average that is updated with events and new information made available is____________.**

a] mater average
b] weighted average
c] moving average
d] mode.

128. **A survey of respondents undertaken at two or more points of time aimed at studying chances over time____________.**

a] multivation effect

b] multi stage sampling
c] longitudinal study
d] focus group study

129. __________ is an experimental error that occurs when respondents react differently to their independent variable on account of earlier measurement.

a] non sampling error
b] inter action error
c] non parametric error
d] non response error

130. In analysis of variance, the mean of all observations across all treatment group is__________.

a] grand mean
b] master average
c] moving average
d] weighted average

131. Scale which does not include an opinion or undecided category and thus requires the respodent to indicate position on the scale is __________.

a] forced choice scale
b] graphic scale
c] scale
d] rating scale

132. A statistical technique used to classify persons or objects into two or more categories on the basis of intervally scaled predicted variables__________.

a] export poto study
b] discriminant analysis
c] goodness of fit
d] inter dependent technique

133. The magnitude of sampling error in the estimate of the parameter that is acceptable to the researcher is ________.

a] allow ask error

b] experimental error

c] tolerance limit

d) standard error

134. A test in which respondents are asked to indicate their preference by using two or more alternatives________.

a] chi square test

b] F-test

c] blind use test

d] grone failed test

135. A sampling in which clusier of elements is the primary sampling instead of individual elements in the population is__________.

a] quota sampling

b] cluster sampling

c] judgement sampling

d] purposive sampling

136. The appropriateness of a measuring instrument for obtaining the desired information is________.

a] Bay rule

b] accuracy

c] cross sectoral study

d] content validity

137. Observation in which the researcher creates the desired situation before observation__________.

a] conditional probability

b] cluster analysis

c] experimetal observation

d] conlrived observation

138. A research dealing with expanding the frontiers of knowledge is___________.

a] fundamental research

b] scientific research

c] qualitative research

d] original research

139. The research that proceeds with a certain problem and specifics alternative solutions is___________.

a] pure research

b] applied research

c] market research

d] value research

140. The research with a class of issues in which several firms may be interested.

a] problem solving

b] problem oriented

c] idea logical

d] solution oriented

141. ____________deals with current information on developments in the macro environment & task environment.

a] Market intelligence system

b] Market research

c] Marketing research

d] Internal accounting system

142. The sharp variations in the demand for goods result in

a] derived demand

b] demand concentration

c] demand validlity

d] industrial demand

143. A chart used to provide time dimension for controlling marketing research is___________.

a] PERT

b] how chart

c] research chart

d] flow chart

144. The storehouse of demographic information can be rightly identified as ___________.

a] syndicated data

b] primary data

c] census data

d] secondary data.

145. ___________utilizes information about individual consumers and allows companies to customize their offerings accordingly.

a] Syndicated services

b] Data base marketing

c] E-marketing

d] Internet marketing.

146. The informal open-ended group discussions that are guided by a trained moderator to focus the discussion on a specific topic are ___________.

a] projected interview

b] informal interview

c] survey

d] focus group interview.

147. The research undertaken to test for cause & effect relationship under enrolled condition is___________.

a] projective technique

b] experimental research

c] observational research

d] case study

148. Observation that are derived from cultural anthropology are called as ___________.

a] ethnography

b] demography

c] psychography

d] physiological

149. The index which shows which customers are more profitable compared to other is ___________.

a] sales index

b] customer index

c] comparative index

d] profitability index

150. Marketing intelligence may be gathered through_________.

a] salesmen

b] field sales managers

c] MIS

d] all of these

151. Who has defined marketing research as systematic objective and exhaustive search for and study of the facts relating to any problem in the field of marketing?

a] Philip Kotler

b] Richard Crisp

c] A.G.R. Delens

d] William Stanton

152. Marketing research helps the firm to acquire better understanding of the___________.

a] consumer

b] competitors

c] marketing environment

d] all the above

153. Market research can be carried out at ____________.

a] consumer level

b] product level

c] market level

d] any of these

154. Marketing research involves research on ____________.

a] markets

b] pricing

c] distribution

d] all the above

155. The technique of interviewing people in central locations such as shopping centre air ports etc is known as ____________.

a] street intercepts

b] side road intercepts

c] mall intercepts

d] central intercept

156. The term used to describe studies commissioned for publicity purposes are known as____________.

a] public research

b] advocacy research

c] directive research

d] image research

157. When performing the situation analysis, it is important to seek information____________.

a] outside of the company

b] inside the company

c] by mailing survey questionnaires to customers

d] by whatever means is practical with anyone who is not connected with the company.

158. A situation analysis is concerned with____________.

a] primary data

b] secondary data

c] tertiary data

d] all of these.

159. During the informal investigation, the researcher talks with:

a] Only those within the company sponsoring the research

b] Those outside the firm who are best qualified to supply information

c] Top management within the sponsoring company

d] All of these.

160. The first step in conducting marketing research is to____________.

a] review sources of data

b] formulate a research design

c] define the problem

d] select the best sources of data.

161. Research used to identify the best approach from among set of alternatives is the ____________.

a] exploratory research

b] primary research

c] secondary research

d] diagnostic research.

ANSWERS

1] a) Laboratory setting observation

2] d) questionnaire

3] d) Dichotomous

4] c) belief

5] b) ordinal scale

6] a) image evaluation

7] b) positioning studies

8] b) to measure consumer preprence for alternate produces

9] b) Graphically portray consumer evaluation of products

10] a) product performance analysis

11] d) deficiences in the nature of sample

12] b) inadequacy of sample

13] a) Uses the same sample over & our again for collection of internaiton

14] d) selection of a quota sample on predetermined parameters

15] d) understanding consumer expectations.

16] b) To improve distribution net worth.

17] b) Market oriented data entrprise

18] c) Marketing Research Advisory Services

19] d) Summarises data non numerically

20] a) A graphical poortriat & consumers evaluation of products

21] c) to gather valuable informaiton for media planning

22] d) purchasing pattern of retallers

23] b) uses the some sample over and over again for collecting the data.

24] a) semantic error

25] b) sampling bias.

26] a) Random sampling

27] d) Area sampling

28] b) involves selectin every nth unit from the population

29] d) yardstick

30] b) precision

31] c) Confidence limit

32] b) Likert scale

33] a) Likert

34] b) opinions & views

35] b) industrial buying guide

36] b) customer data base
37] b) customer data base
38] d) data mining
39] b) no of territories to be visited
40] d) geographical grouping of customers
41] b) Televisions rating point
42] b) TRP
43] a) Russel Colley
44] c) Delphi method
45] b) Nicosia model
46] c) focus group
47] c) behavoural research
48] a) exprimental research
49] c) rating scale
50] d) Rating scale
51] a) Simple random sample
52] d) stratified random
53] c) convenience sample
54] a) judgement sample
55] c) scientific method
56] b) Healthy skepticism
57] d) multiple regression analysis
58] c) factor analysis
59] d) cluster analysis
60] d) product pretest model
61] a) queuing model
62] a) game theory
63] a) conjoint analysis
64] c) descriptive research
65] b) exploratory research
66] b) exploratory research
67] a) Primary data
68] d) Consumer panel research

69] b) attitude
70] b) state of being
71] c) PERT
72] b) empiricalevidence
73] c) decision tree approach
74] c) sales analysis
75] d) longitudinal study
76] a) secondary data
77] a) observation method
78] b) attitudinal study
79] a) interval scale
80] c) sampling frame
81] d) sales analysis by size of order
82] c) image evaluation study
83] a) hypothesis
84] c) causal research
85] a) secondary data
86] d) Linear
87] b) Ordinal scale
88] d) represents the true differneces in chracteristic under study
89] b) predictive validity
90] b) concurrent validity
91] d) paired comparision scale
92] d) Thurstone rating scale
93] a) multiple sampling
94] b) systematic sampling
95] c) population is divided into mutially exclusive strate
96] c) quota sampling
97] b) judgement sample
98] b) panelsamples
99] d) hypothesis
100] c) experimental error

101] b) performance analysis
102] c) market patential
103] d) jury of executives
104] a) delphi method
105] b) econometric model
106] a) brain storming
107] c) monadic test
108] d) Business model building
109] b) word association test
110] b) thematic appreciation test
111] b) comparitive sampling
112] b) soloman's four group design
113] b) snow ball design
114] c) Price index
115] d) sampling frame
116] b) sampling distribution
117] a) recall test
118] c) status bias
119] b) WAT
120] a) rating scale
121] b) Omnibus panel
122] c) Likert hypothesis
123] c) non response error
124] a) ordinal scale
125] d) multiple regression
126] c) experimental error
127] a) matter average
128] a) multivariation effect
129] c) non parametric error
130] b) master average
131] a) forced choice scale
132] c) goodness of fit
133] d) standard error

134] c) blind use test
135] b) cluster sumpling
136] d) content validity
137] d) controlled observation
138] a) fundamental research
139] b) applied research
140] d) solution oriented
141] a) marketing research
142] a) derived demand
143] d) flow chart
144] c) census data
145] a) syndicated services
146] d) focus group interview
147] b) experimental research
148] a) enthnography
149] b) customer index
150] d) all of these
151] b) Richard crisp
152] d) all the above
153] d) any of these
154] d) all the above
155] d) centrial intercept
156] b) advocacy research
157] b) inside the company
158] d) All of these
159] b) those outside the firm who are best qualified to supply information
160] d) select the best sources of data
161] a) Exploratory research.

10

INTERNATIONAL TRADE

1. **The fourth round of ministerial conference of WTO was held at _________.**
   a] Doha
   b] Dublin
   c] Dunkark
   d] Delhi

2. **MFN stands for __________.**
   a] Market For National Products
   b] Market Friendly Nations
   c] Most Friendly Nations
   d] Most Favored Nations

3. **Euro Bank notes are issued from _________.**
   a] 1st Jan 2000
   b] 1st Jan 2001
   c] 1st Jan 2002
   d] 1st Jan 1999

4. **Accounting unit of IMF is _________.**
   a] Dollar
   b] SDR
   c] Yen
   d] Euro

5. **WEO stands for _________.**
   a] World Economic Outlook
   b] World Economic Outcome
   c] World Efficiency Outlook
   d] World estimate of origin.

6. **Domestic country means_________.**
   a] the country of origin
   b] the poor countries
   c] country with poor marketing system.
   d] land locked countries.

7. **Domestic company is a company _________.**
   a] selling a products to poor country
   b] selling products in a specific trade zone
   c] company operating within the national boundaries
   d] company that is not selling in the country of it or its origin

8. **The companies locating the branch in the foreign markets are_________.**
   a] transnational company
   b] international company
   c] multinational Company
   d] global Company

9. **Extending the domestic product, price & promotion to foreign market is an example of_________.**
   a] Multinational
   b] International
   c] Transnational
   d] Global Company

10. A company produces products in one country & markets in the entire world is _________.

a] Transnational

b] Multinational

c] Global

d] International

11. A Company having multiple points of production, investments and operation is called as_________.

a] Global

b] Transnational

c] International

d] Multinational

12. Dr. Reddy a pharma company that produces in India & sells world over is an example of _________.

a] Domestic Company

b] Multinational Company

c] Global Company

d] Transnational Company

13. If Toyota manufactures cars in Japan & sells it world over then it is a _________.

a] Multinational company

b] Global Company

c] Transnational Company

d] Domestic Company

14. TATA produces car in India sells in India then it is a_________.

a] Domestic Company

b] Global Company

c] Transnational Company

d] International Company

15. European & American oil Companies prefer to establish the oil exploration plants in Gulf due to _________.

a] cultural ability

b] avoid tarrifs

c] near ness to raw material

d] increase in market share

16. Mobil oil establishes its refinery facilities in areas near by its point of distribution to gain advantages of _________.

a] nearness to raw material

b] avoid tarrifs

c] avoid high cost of transport

d] to increase market share

17. Companies like Sony or Honda prefer direct investment to go globally due to_________.

a] high cost of transport

b] avoid tarrifs & import quotas

c] availability of quality human resources

d] availability of managerial competence

18. Most of the Japanese firm entered US & European markets due to _________.

a] political stability

b] severe home competition

c] limited home market

d] availability of technology

19. Geocentric approach emphasises on_________.

a] exporting to the neighbouring countries

b] select the employees from the native globe & operate with a number of subsidiary

c] company establishes a foreign subsidiary

d] presumes that foreign market is extension of local market.

20. Comparative cost theory is coined by__________.

a] A. G. Pigou

b] Robbins

c] Alfred marshall

d] David Ricardo

21. The countries in the long run will tend to specialise in the business of goods in those business where they enjoy low cost advantage is __________.

a] opportunity cost theory

b] comparative cost

c] modern theory of international trade

d] theory of dissolute difference in cost.

22. The comparative cost theory is based on the presumption that __________.

a] efficient allocation of resources promotes global trade

b] perfect competition exists in international markets

c] every country requires some commodities to be imported.

d] the only element of cost of production is labor

23. The derived advantage of comparative cost theory is__________.

a] to provide a valid basis to international trade

b] the only element of cost of production is labor

c] these are no trade barriers

d] efficient allocation of global resources

24. The opportunity cost theory is provided by -

a] Adam smith

b] Gottlried Haberler

c] Bertliohlin

d] David Ricardo

25. ——— provided basis for international business in terms of exporting a particular product than a group of other products.

a] Opportunity cost theory

b] Comparative cost theory

c] Absolute difference in cost theory

d] A reciprocal demand theory

26. The theory that provides a basis for international business of exporting a product to a particular country than to a group countries is_________.

a] the went for surplus theory

b] reciprocal demand theory

c] opportunity cost theory

d] absolute difference in cost

27. The theory of factor endowment is based on the presumption that __________.

a] factor of production are perfectly mobile within each country

b] every country should specialise in producing a particular product of least cost

c] the only element of cost is labor

d] different prevailing endowment of the factors of production

28. Factors supplier are fixed in each country is the assumption of _________.

a] Heckseher Ohlin theory

b] Ricardian theory

c] Golt tried Haberler theory

d] Smith's theory

29. Who said every country should specalise in producing those products which it can produce at least cost than other countries & exchange those products with other products?

a] Adam smith

b] David Ricardo

c] Ohlin

d] J.S. Mill

30. Who coined the concept of reciprocal demand?

a] H. Myinr

b] J.J. Mill

c] David Ricardo

d] Adam smith

31. Who said, whether the advantage which one country has over another be natural or acquired is of no consequence?

a] Bertliohlin

b] Haberler

c] Smith

d] Ricardo

32. The managerial decision made by analyzing the significance of data of threats & opportunities in the environments is termed as__________.

a] Environmental diagnosis

b] Environmental development

c] Environmental scruting

d] Environmental protection

33. Trade unions is __________.

a] political factor

b] internal factor

c] external factor

d] cultural factor

34. A set of traditional beliefs and values which are transmitted and shared in a given society is ________.

a] life style

b] values

c] culture

d] ideologies

35. When a foreign culture is observed by making reference to personal and cultural values it is called as ________.

a] value analysis

b] self reference criteria

c] ideological crisis

d] cultural attitude

36. Cultures which handle information in a direct & linear fashion are called as ________.

a] polychromic

b] monochromic

c] high context culture

d] universal culture

37. The culture in which people work on several firm simultenuously instead of persuing single firm it is ________.

a] dynamic culture

b] universal culture]

c] monochromic

d] polychromic

38. The system under which customer allocates resources considering his choice of production is ________.

a] capitalistic

b] socialistic

c] communistic

d] mixed

39. The common needs in the people irrespective of race, religion, caste, creed, etc. are termed as__________.

a] cultural universal

b] non- prolific culture

c] high context culture

d] polychromic

40. The process of nationalization of property without compensation is __________.

a] domestication

b] nationalization

c] expropriation

d] contiscation

41. Situation where foreign business firms relinquish control & ownership in favour of domestic investors__________.

a] nationalization

b] domestication

c] expropriation

d] confiscation

42. A political system where only one party dominates the country is __________.

a] multi party system

b] monopoly party system

c] single party system

d] two party system

43. The risk due to imposition of controls on the foreign business operation is __________.

a] financial risk

b] operation risk

c] cultural risk

d] trade risk

44. The training institutes that develop people for employment in select professions is called as _________.

a] head hunting

b] body shopping

c] walk in

d] consult in

45. When parent country nationals are selected for all the key management job it is called as _________.

a] poiycentric approach

b] geocentric approach

c] activity centric approach

d] ethnocentric approach

46. When all key job are assigned to the host country nationals it is called as_________.

a] polycentric approach

b] ethnocentric approach

c] geo centric approach

d] activity centric

47. The training that provides the reasons for the behaviour of the people of the host country is_________.

a] attribution training

b] cultural awareness training

c] cognitive behaviour modification training

d] experimental training

48. The training that provides information regarding behaviour practices which results in setting rewards or punishments in host country is _________.

a] cultural awareness training

b] cognitive behavioural modification training

c] attribution training

d] experimental training.

49. The major focus of relationship marketing is on________.

a] customer retention
b] short time scale
c] focus on single scale
d] limited commitment

50. The marketing which is carried out by companies for hiring people is ________.

a] supplier marketing
b] influence marketing
c] referral marketing
d] recruitment marketing

51. The most important feature of mission statement is_________.

a] understand what business you are in
b] identify consumer needs
c] week a broad ideas
d] define target market.

52. The segmentation that focuses on the type of usage pattern is _________.

a] benefit segmentation
b] demographic segmentation
c] psycho graphic segmentation
d] usage segmentation

53. When did the International Monetary Fund (IMF) begin its operations?

a] 1945
b] 1946
c] 1947
d] 1948

54. When was the first amendment to the articles of the IMF made which led to the creation of the special Drawing Rights (SDR) facility?

a] 1969

b] 1971

c] 1975

d] 1978

55. When was the Uruguay Round of multilateral trade negotiations under the GATT launched ?

a] January 1986

b] June 1986

c] September 1986

d] December 1986

56. In which year did the European Economic Community (EEC), popularly known as the, European Common Market (ECM), come into existence?

a] 1956 b] 1958

c] 1960 d] 1962

57. When was the "Group of 77, (an economic group of the Third World countries to protect the economic and trade interests of developing countries) formed under the auspices of the United Nations?

a] 1962 b] 1964

c] 1966 d] 1968

58. Which country is OPEC's largest oil exporter?

a] Saudi Arabia

b] Iraq

c] Kuwait

d] United Arab Emirates.

59. International trade must exist because of ________.

a] political factors

b] differences in resources

c] economic consideration

d] all of those

60. ______ is the adaptation of the domestic marketing mix suitable to the marketing differences in market environment in each country of operation.

a] Global marketing

b] Multinational marketing

c] International marketing

d] Export marketing

61. ______ views different set of a country's market as a unit for identifying groups of prospective buyers with similar needs

a] Global marketing

b] International marketing

c] Export marketing

d] Multinational marketing

62. Chinar Food Products India is selling "Druk" fruit juices of Bhutan in India it is an example of __________.

a] direct export

b] indirect export

c] licencing

d] franchising

63. Coca-Cola is sold and distributed in India under ________.

a] licencing agreement

b] franchising

c] assembly

d] indirect export

64. When two firms pool their resources directly in a collaboration that goes beyond the lines of a joint venture is__________.

a] merger b] acquisition

c] take over d] strategic alliance

65. Mc Donald's and Pepsi are the examples of _________.

a] local brands

b] family brands

c] universal brands

d] distributors brands

66. The company involved in the export of surplus to other country without direct marketing efforts in the foreign market is in _________.

a] export marketing

b] international marketing

c] domestic marketing

d] multinational marketing

67. ITPO stands for _________.

a] Indian Trade Position Organization

b] International Trade & Promotional organization

c] India Tarrif & Ports Organization

d] Indian Trade Promotion Organization

ANSWERS

1] a) Doha

2] d) Most Favoured Nations

3] b) 1st Jan. 2001

4] b) SDR

5] a) World Economci Outlook

6] a) Country of origin
7] c) company opirating within national boundries
8] b) International company
9] b) Intrnational
10] b) Multinational
11] b) Transnational
12] b) multinational
13] a) multinational company
14] a) Domestic
15] c) nearness to naw material
16] c) avoid high cot of transport
17] b) avoid tariffs and import quotas.
18] c) limited home market
19] b) Select the employees from the globe and operate with no of subsidiary
20] d) David Ricardo
21] b) Comparitive cost
22] d) the only element of cost of production is labour
23] b) the only element of cost of production is labor
24] b) Gottlried Haberler
25] d) A reciprocal demand theory
26] d) absolute difference in cost
27] d) Different prevoiling endowment of the factors of production.
28] a) Heckseher Ohlin theory
29] c) Ohlin
30] b) J.S. Mill
31] c) Smith
32] a) Environemnt Diagnosis.
33] b) Internal factor
34] c) culture
35] b) Self reference criteria.
36] b) monochromic
37] c) monochromic
38] a) capitalistic
39] b) non-prolific culture

40] b) nationalisation
41] b) domestication
42] b) nonopoly party system
43] a) financial risk
44] b) body shopping
45] d) Ethnocentric approach
46] a) Polycentric approach
47] c) cognitive behaviour modification training
48] a) Cultural awareness training
49] a) customer retention
50] d) recruitment marketing
51] a) understand what business you are in
52] d) usage segmentation
53] a) 1945
54] a) 1969
55] c) Sept 1986
56] b) 1958
57] b) 1964
58] a) Saudi Arabia
59] d) All of these
60] b) multinational marketing
61] a) global marketing
62] c) licensing
63] a) licencing agreement
64] d) strategic alliance
65] c) Universal brands
66] a) Exportmarketing
67] d) Indian Trade promotion Organisation

11

E-MARKETING

1. **E-marketing involves use of information technology and electronic devices for ___________.**
   a] selling to ultimate consumers.
   b] developing marketing techniques.
   c] developing marketing strategies.
   d] developing marketing strategies and creating exchanges.

2. **Use of telephone, fax, television, mobile & modem for marketing is called _______ marketing.**
   a] audio-visual
   b] cyber
   c] digital
   d] electronic

3. **Customers are reluctant to use credit cards on line & thus marketers use _______ to protect information in transit.**
   a] proxy servers
   b] filtering
   c] coding
   d] encryption algorithms

4. **Two e-marketing communication technologies used to track user behavior on the web are ___________.**
   a] Log files & cookies
   b] Web language & standard.

c] Inter transfer & web data.

d] Ad banners & pops.

5. Log files & Cookies help in relationship marketing through ________.

a] customizing products & services.

b] providing web securities

c] developing web sites

d] presenting ads.

6. Key ethical issue in using e-marketing is concerned with ________.

a] protection of copyrights

b] use of consumer information

c] protection of trademark

d] unethical ads

7. An important advantage that arises from using online survey is ________.

a] respondents authenticity

b] less biased

c] broad reach

d] easy tabulation

8. When individuals forward e-mail to friends, co-workers, family etc, they are participating in __________.

a] Internet- marketing

b] Web-marketing

c] Viral-marketing

d] SMS-marketing

9. What are the media vehicles used in internet advertising?

a] E-mail and websites

b] E-mail, websites and wireless content sponsorship

c] Web sites and wireless content sponsorship

d] Web sites and web-contents

10. What are the factors to be taken into accounts for e-media buying?

a] Cost per thousand and cost per action

b] Active viewing and flexibility

c] E-mail list and technology

d] Price and public relations

11. What is the most popular online activity among Indian users?

a] Surf local sites

b] E-mail

c] Surf local and foreign sites

d] Download

12. _____ is an intermediary firm that buys products and resells them online.

a] e-retailer

b] e-agent

c] e-tailer

d] e-distribution

13. An e-marketer should take care of ___________ as it could irritate and annoy users of web

a] Spam

b] Spam filters

c] Spider

d] Spot

14. A free monthly e-mail newsletter distributed world wide is ________.

a] Web Marketing Today

b] Web selling Today

c] Web Distribution Today

d] Web Retailer Today

15. **Kiosk based computer interviewing is an innovative way of gathering ________.**
   a] advertising recall
   b] media effectiveness
   c] customer feedback
   d] retailer feedback

16. **Which is internet's largest advertising company?**
   a] Zed dust
   b] Demon Internet
   c] Double Click
   d] Ad Décor .com

17. **________ is database which is usually subject oriented, smaller & applicable to a single business unit or department like HR, marketing etc.**
   a] Data warehouse
   b] Data mining
   c] Data marts
   d] Data universe

18. **________ is a data analysis tool which relates to use of automated process which help in discovering patterns in a data set.**
   a] Data mining
   b] Data warehouse
   c] Data marts
   d] Data universe

19. **__________ tool enables the marketer to establish content & execution of direct marketing initiatives.**
   a] Interaction Management
   b] Media Management
   c] Direct Marketing Management
   d] Campaign Management

20. Tim Berners-Lee conceived the World Wide Web & released it to the public domain in ______.

a] 1991

b] 1990

c] 1992

d] 1993

21. ______ has been defined as the sale of goods & services via Internet or other electronic channels for personal or household use of consumers.

a] E-marketing

b] E-retailing

c] E-selling

d] E-intermediary

22. An important advantage of e-selling over face to face selling is ___________.

a] Lack of legal formalities.

b] Large customer base.

c] After sale care

d] Larger profits.

23. The worlds largest & most successful e-retailer of books is ________.

a] Fig Leaves.com

b] Kazaamedia.com

c] Amazon.com

d] E-Bay. Com

24. The worlds largest e-grocer is ________.

a] Tesco.com

b] Boots.com

c] Netshop.com

d.Quillcorp.com

25. _________ is a pop-up that appears while downloading a web site.

a] Banner

b] Interstitial

c] Meta ad

d] Sponsorship

26. The E-Bay .Co.UK is a significant, profitable & successful e-commerce site which is known for its _____.

a] auctions

b] direct marketing

c] credit sales

d] premium priced products

27. The emerging wireless electronic shopping is called ___________.

a] e-shopping

b] e-retailing

c] e-selling

d] m-shopping

28. Companies that supply products & services directly to individual businesses are ___________.

a] e-dealers

b] e-distributors

c] e-wholesaler

d] e-retailer

29. Companies that help in linking other businesses and take a commission or fees of any business that occurs via the link are called ________.

a] matchmaker

b] infomediary

c] mercantile agent
d] e-broker

30. A company whose business is based on gathering information about consumers & selling it to other businesses is called ________.

a] e-market research
b] infomediary
c] e-research agency
d] e-professional

31. When retailer pays rent for permit to sell online under a mall's umbrella, it is called ________.

a] online mall
b] catalog mall
c] rent-a-mall
d] umbrella mall

32. Companies that have network of physical retail stores & have introduced online offerings are called ________.

a] Offline & online retailer
b] Online retailer
c] Online supermarket
d] Clicks & mortar

33. In permission marketing strategy when consumers agree to receive information & promotional message from marketers they decide to ________.

a] Message-in
b] Receive-in
c] Opt-in
d] Sign- in

34. When one web site agrees to pay another web site a commission for new business opportunities due to referrals by the other site it is called as ________.

a] Affiliate marketing

b] Referral marketing

c] Commission marketing

d] Mutual marketing

35. A banner ad displays an ad in a rectangular box at the ________ of a computer screen.

a] top

b] top or bottom

c] centre

d] bottom

36. A permanent banner ad is called ________.

a] Button

b] Icon

c] pop-up

d] Full banner

37. A technique that is used to authenticate e-documents is called ________.

a] digital stamp

b] e-signatures

c] digital signatures

d] typed signatures

38. ________ is a card that not only help in e-transaction but also store & process more information & interact with electronic devices.

a] Smart cards

b] Credit cards

c] Debit cards

d] ATM cards

39. E-mail services, electronic greetings, chat software & software for net are called ________.

a] Nettish products

b] e-products

c] e-commerce

d] e-goods & services

40. The advantage of e-marketing to consumers:

a] Round the clock shopping

b] In-depth product information

c] Easy to place order & quick delivery

d] All the above

41. _______ is a web site address used to identify an Internet location.

a] E-trade mark

b] Domain name

c] Dot com

d] E-address

42. Bababazaar.com is the first Indian e- commerce site offering convenience to order_______.

a] books

b] fresh vegetables

c] e- greetings

d] toys

43. Pitara .com is India's first site designed for _______.

a] children

b] teenagers

c] adults

d] elders

44- _______ is software on the hard drive of an online shopper which can hold credit cards in encrypted form.

a] Web wallet

b] Internet Wallet

c] Direct Wallet

d] Digital wallet

45-On line catalogues is an instrument of _______.

a] advertising

b] distribution

c] data base

d] payment

46-________ refers to any scheme that allows a person to pay for products by transmitting a number from one computer to another.

a] Digital cash

b] Internet cash

c] Digital credit

d] Digital delivery

47. A text that is not constrained to be sequential is ______.

a] code text b] basic text

c] technical text d] hyper text

48. The protocol responsible for transferring transmission & display of web page is ________.

a] web page b] HTTP

c] IP d] DNS

49. Click & mortar is the term related with __________ operations of internet.

a] Global reach b] 24X7 operation

c] Lowest d] easy to handle

50. The major difficulty in commercialization of E-Commerce is ________.

a] difficult to calculate ROI
b] difficult to reach potential customer
c] poor delivery system
d] high maintenance cost

51. The E- procurement solution offered by ITC is ________.

a] E- distribution b] E- governance
c] E- chaupal d] E- system

52. Amazon com is an example of ______.

a] B2B b] B2G c] B2C d] C2B

53. Price- discovery mechanism is the speciality of ______.

a] Transaction model
b] brokerage model
c] Community model
d] affiliate model

54. The major disadvantage of traditional marketing to E-marketing is ______.

a] expensive & time consuming
b] simplicity
c] no ethical barriers
d] no regulation

55. The facility to use power of online net works & computer communication in marketing is

a] Quiche marketing b] Techno marketing
c] system marketing d] online marketing

56. Home computer users wired up to commercial online services & the internet are ____.

a] commercial consumer b] E-consumers

c] data users d] E-beneficiary

57. ________ is the basic feature of Data Warehouse

a] Transformation of data b] Subject oriented data

c] Standard reporting system d] Data mining

58. The item in the balance scorecard which is cascaded down at lower levels is _______.

a] KM Index b] Virtual index

c] subject index d] data index

59. A service that gives freedom to the customer to tailor the services as per his choice is ____.

a] customer orientation b] customer friendly

c] customization d] creative customer service

60. The delivery of time sensitive information personalized to each customer is ____.

a] Recommendation b] Narrow casting

c] Customer interaction d] Time trance analysis

61. _______ is an online scam where the senders try to cheat customers by asking them to disclose financial /credit related information.

a] Phishing b] Copyright breach

c] Nigerian scam d] Credit scam

62. The science of encryption is termed as

a] cryptography b] cryptology

c] cypherology d] cyber science

63. A third party who holds an auction on buyer's payment, until the buyer received the purchased item offers __________.

a] E trailer b] E scrow service

c] mail payment service d] cyber squatting

64. A trademarks ________ violation that involves the registration of domain that resemble or duplicate the names of existing corporations.

a] cyber squatting b] cyber marking

c] Elector copy mark d] encryption breach

65.________ is an auction in which bidding begins at a high price & drops till a bidder accepts the price.

a] French auction b] Dutch auction

c] English auction d] regular auction

66. An e-commerce utility that keeps track of selected items of purchase & accumulates the purchase for one time payment is called __________.

a] Shopping cart b] shopping mail

c] shopping lobby d] quick shop

67. Marketing tactics that rely on existing customers to tell others about company's products is called ______.

a] Viral marketing

b] virtual marketing

c] collection marketing

d] Bargain & sprayed

68. A model on which multiple on line merchants are hosted on a website:

a] Web mall b] Electronic mall

c] Virtual mall d] Uni mall

69. __________ is a facility that manages the transfer of funds from a customer to the merchant of an e-commerce site.

a] Web Payment Service

b] Mail Payment Service

c] E-service

d] E-scroll service

70. _________ is used by e-marketers to study the proportion of users viewing an ad after clicking on it.

a] Click stream analysis

b] Click tracking

c] Click ad rate

d] Click through rate

ANSWERS

1] d) developing marketing strategies and creating exchanges

2] d) electronic marketing

3] d) Encryption algorithms

4] a) Log files & Cookies

5] a) Customizing products & services

6] b) use of consumer information

7] d) easy tabulation

8] c) Viral marketing

9] b) E-mail, websites and wireless content sponsorship

10] a) Cost per thousand and cost per action

11] b) E-mail

12] c) e-tailer

13] a) spam

14] a) Web Marketing Today

15] c) customer feedback

16] c) Double Click

17] c) Data Marts
18] a) Data mining
19] d) Campaign management
20] a) 1991
21] b) E- retailing
22] b) large customer base
23] c) Amazon .com
24] a) Tesco.com
25] b) interstitials
26] a) auction
27] d) m-shopping
28] b) e-distributor
29] a) matchmaker
30] b) infomediary
31] a) online mall
32] d) Clicks & Mortar
33] c.) opt-in
34] a) affiliate marketing
35] b) top or bottom
36] a) button
37] c) digital signatures
38] a) Smart card
39] a) Nettish products
40] d) All the above
41] b) Domain name
42] b) fresh vegetables
43] a) children
44] d) Digital wallet
45] a) advertising
46] a) Digital cash
47] d) hyper text
48] b) HTTP

49] a) Global reach
50] c) poor delivery system
51] c) e-chaupal
52] c) B2C
53] a) Traction model
54] a) expensive & time consuming
55] d) online marketing
56] b) e-consumer
57] b) subject oriented
58] a) KM Index
59] c) customization
60] b) narrow casting
61] a) phishing
62] b) cryptology
63] b) *E scrow service*
64] a) cyber squatting
65] b) Dutch auction
66] a) shopping cart
67] a) viral marketing
68] c) Virtual mal
69] a) Web payment Service
70] d) Click through rate

12

APPLICATION ORIENTED QUESTIONS

1. **In Indian context rural marketing plays the role of__________.**
   a] concept Marketing
   b] develop Marketing
   c] idea Marketing
   d] infrastructural development

2. **The key point in rural distribution in the Indian context can be __________.**
   a] Melas
   b] Hatts
   c] Village shop
   d] Mobile vans

3. **Low priced pouched packs offered to rural consumers is an example of__________.**
   a] Trial & error method
   b] Try & promote concept
   c] Try & adopt concept
   d] Product idea relation

4. **Thomson rural index is used in Indian context for__________.**

a] product differentiation
b] segmentation
c] promotion media election
d] ·market identification

5. **Brand Acquisition Fund is created by Government of India for __________.**
a] to provide capital to Indian firms
b] to provide funds to Indian firms
c] to promote Indian Brand
d] top promote Indian MNC's

6. **Respect culture, custom & language of the country of trade & be a good corporate citizen is a principle called as__________.**
a] Sony formula
b] IBM way
c] Matsushita Prescription
d] Ford & Idea

7. **The equivalent to ISO 9000 is __________.**
a] ISO14000
b] EURO-2000
c] Bharat-2000
d] Bharat-II

8. **ISPAT Group belongs to __________.**
a] Ruia b] Birlas
c] Mittal d] Jain

9. **The most important feature of a global firm is__________.**
a] advantage of scale economy
b] presence in many countries
c] heavy capital investment
d] latest technology

10. Which Indian industry has competitive advantage in international trade?

a] Textiles

b] Pharma

c] Industrial goods

d] Food products

11. The Global competitiveness reports are released by________.

a] WTO

b] WER

c] VHIDO

d] VHDF

12. The Taj West End's effort to offer time bound service to its customer is an example of__________.

a] time dimension differentiation

b] service dimension differentiation

c] utility dimension differentiation

d] differentiation on the basis of people

13. Using Icons like Sharukh Khan, Karishma Kapoor Airlel uses the concept of ____________.

a] differentiating by people

b] differentiating by quality

c] differentiating by Image

d] differentiating by service

14. The example of syndicated research service is ___________.

a] motivation research

b] concept evaluation

c] MRS

d] MRAS

13

PRACTICAL QUESTIONS

1. **Offering sundry banking facility by ABN AMRO is an example of__________.**
   a] value communication
   b] value creation
   c] value selection
   d] value proposition

2. **Offering a global credit facility by Standard Chartered Bank to all card holders is an example of__________.**
   a] value communication
   b] value delivery
   c] value preposition
   d] value enhancement

3. **In order to know how information technology industry is performing the marketing manager has to perform_______.**
   a] sectoral analysis
   b] key area analysis
   c] economy analysis
   d] industry analysis

4. **To know the performance of economy and its projection over a period of years one should go for__________.**
   a] SWOT analysis
   b] economy analysis

c] CBA analysis
d] industry analysis

5. **Demographic environment is the part of _________.**
a] economic environment
b] competitive environment
c] socio-cultural environment
d] mega environment

6. **A company involved in business of selling FMCG products must undertake analysis of_________.**
a] political environment
b] technological environment
c] industry
d] consumers

7. **A steel industry demanding protection from external competition indicates _________.**
a] sectoral protection
b] economic protection
c] corporate protection
d] technology protection

8. **Lowering of trade/ import tariff is the example of_________.**
a] macro-economic reform
b] trade policy reform
c] structural adjustments
d] micro-economic reforms

9. **Curtailment of public sector is a part of_________.**
a] the new industrial policy
b] new trade policy
c] new banking & fiscal policy
d] FERA liberalization

10. **Market driven pricing is an example of_________.**
a] structural adjustments
b] banking reforms
c] exit policy
d] fiscal reforms

11. The take over code was introduced by__________.

a] SEBI
b] MRTP Commission
c] Planning Commission
d] NRF

12. NRF stands for__________.

a] National Reconstruction Fund
b] National Renewal Fund
c] National Recycling Fund
d] National Redemption Fund

13. The global partner of UTI is__________.

a] Prudential of UK
b] ABN Amro
c] Orix Corporation Japan
d] Alliance Capital USA

14. The global partner of ICICI is__________.

a] Lazaro Brothers of UK
b] Asian Capital Hongkong
c] Prudential of UK
d] Temple for worldwide

15. Variety and flexibility in production is an example of__________.

a] backup strategy
b] competitive advantage
c] core competence
d] product strategy

16. The low cost advantage in production enjoyed by SONY over others is an example of__________.

a] competitive advantage
b] backup strategy
c] core competence
d] product strategy

17. **Differentiation is a source of competitive advantage in_________.**
    a] finance
    b] human resources
    c] R & D
    d] marketing

18. **Leverage & gearing are the sources of competitive advantages in_________.**
    a] marketing
    b] finance
    c] operations
    d] R & D

19. **Comparing a Ford Taurus car with its competitors to prove its superiority is_________.**
    a] strategy
    b] benchmarking
    c] competitive strategy
    d] value analysis

20. **Videocon TV buying Uptron color picture tube unit is an example of_________.**
    a] value chain analysis
    b] competitive advantage
    c] integration
    d] merger

21. **'Maggi' of Nestle is an example of_________.**
    a] competitive advantage through brand power
    b] value addition
    c] value enhancement
    d] core competence

22. **Dupont's unique strength in chemical technology is an example of_________.**
    a] competitive advantage
    b] value addition
    c] core competence
    d] strategic power

23. Exclusive retail outlet idea of Vimal is an example of__________.

a] value addition
b] promotion strategy
c] positioning
d] effective marketing strategy

24. Dettol's claim of providing total protection from germs is__________.

a] differentiated product
b] customized product
c] augmented product
d] branded product

25. Aristocrat introducing suitcases with wheels is an example of__________.

a] potential product
b] augmented product
c] customized product
d] differentiated product

26. Low priced 'PARKER' pen is an example of __________.

a] stretching down
b] stretching up
c] line filling
d] line stretching

27. Philips introducing a high priced 'POWERPLAY' is an example of__________.

a] stretching up
b] line filling
c] line stretching
d] line pruning

28. Close up with gel is an example of__________.

a] differentiation based on packaging
b] differentiation based on ingredients
c] differentiation based on functional value
d] differentiation based on additional feature

29. Vatika with herbal ingredients is an example of_________.

a] differentiation based on packaging
b] differentiation based on ingredients
c] differentiation based on additional value
d] differentiation based on functional value

30. 3M Scotch Magic tape is an example of_________.

a] differentiation based on packaging
b] differentiation based on ingredients
c] differentiation based on functional value
d] differentiation based on additional value

31. The Citi Banks ad for superior "Business Traveller" options is an example of_________.

a] Product positioning
b] Value proposition
c] Product differentiation
d] Competitive advantage

32. The Avis slogan "Avis is the company who will provide the best service" is an example of

a] product utility
b] value proposition
c] brand position
d] product differentiation

33. Positioning of Maruti Omni as a high space snd low priced and multi -purpose van is an example of _________.

a] brand positioning
b] product positioning
c] repositioning
d] product differentiation

34. Ad stating milkmaid as an ingredient for a variety of sweets for all uses involving milk is an example of_________.

a] product differentiation
b] brand positioning
c] product positioning
d] brand repositioning

35. The brand name 'Walkman' indicates _________.
a] distinctiveness
b] name communicating function
c] use of company name
d] appeal

36. AMUL as a brand name indicates_________.
a] company name
b] attributes of the product
c] acronym
d] function

37. 'Nestle' is an example of_________.
a] individual brand name
b] umbrella brand
c] company name as brand name
d] store brand

38. LAKME is an example of_________.
a] family brand
b] umbrella brand
c] company name
d] individual brand

39. MAGGI is an example of_________.
a] family brand
b] company brand
c] brand extension
d] private label

40. SURF is an example of_________.
a] category extension
b] brand rejuvenation
c] line extension
d] brand relaunch

41. P&G's relaunch of VICKS as New Vicks Vaporub is an example of__________.

a] brand relaunch
b] brand extension
c] brand proliferation
d] brand rejuvenation

42. High price paid for acquisition of Translektra by Godrej is an example of__________.

a] Brand acquisition
b] Brand equity
c] Brand proliferation
d] Brand development

43. 'Philips' having a separate corner for its products in a super bazar is an example of __________.

a] exclusive retailing
b] shop in shop
c] franchising
d] showroom

44 'AMWAY' is an example of__________.

a] direct marketing
b] franchising
c] direct selling
d] non store retailing

45 Modicare is an example of__________.

a] MLM b] direct selling
c] home selling d] franchising

46 'KIDS KEMP' is an example of__________.

a] civil supply stores
b] retail outlet
c] departmental store
d] super market

47 'Cross roads' is an example of________.

a] shopping malls

b] retail chain

c] discount chain

d] departmental stores

48. **The Nilgiris is an example of________.**

a] departmental store

b] franchisee store

c] retail chain

d] mall

49. **Otto Berlington is an example of________.**

a] franchisee store

b] direct mail marketing

c] catalogue marketing

d] database marketing

50. **Asian Sky Shop is an example of________.**

a] direct marketing

b] home selling

c] direct response marketing

d] telemarketing

51. **Allowing a customer to book a cinema ticket through internet is an example of________.**

a] web marketing

b] tele marketing

c] e-Commerce

d] convenience marketing

52. **Pricing of BPL TV at Rs 7500 is an example of________.**

a] psychological pricing

b] key factor pricing

c] tender pricing

d] differentiated pricing

53. **New Sundrop Oil for heart care & vitamins is an example of________.**

a] psychological appeal

b] rational appeal
c] fear appeal
d] message appeal

54. 'Love at first bite' is an example of________.
a] emotional appeal
b] message appeal
c] humor appeal
d] fear appeal

55. Free Ray-Ban glasses with Suzuki Shogun is an example of____ ______.
a] coupons b] gift
c] premium d] discount

56. Rs.150 off on a new Hawkins in exchange for any old pressure cooker is an example of________.
a] installment
b] coupon
c] price off
d] exchange scheme

57 'Lakme create your own shade' is an example of__________.
a] contest b] gift
c] premium d] special offer

ANSWERS

1] d] value proposition
2] b] value delivery
3] d] industry analysis
4] b] economy analysis
5] d] mega environment
6] d] consumers
7] c] corporate protection
8] b] Trade Policy Reform
9] a] The new industrial policy
10] a] structural adjustments

11] a] SEBI
12] b] National Renewal Fund
13] b] ABN Amro
14] c] Prudential of UK
15] b] Competitive advantage
16] a] Competitive advantage
17] d] Marketing
18] b] finance
19] b] benchmarking
20] c] integration
21] a] Competitive advantage through brand power
22] c] Core competence
23] c] Positioning
24] a] differentiated product
25] b] Augmented product
26] a] stretching down
27] a] stretching up
28] b] differentiation based on ingredients
29] b] differentiation based on ingredients
30] c] differentiation based on functional value
31] d] competitive advantage
32] b] value proposition
33] a] brand positioning
34] d] brand repositioning
35] b] name communicating function
36] c] acronym
37] a] individual brand name
38] b] umbrella brand
39] c] brand extension
40] c] line extension
41] d] brand rejuvenation
42] b] brand equity
43] b] shop in shop
44] a] direct marketing

45] a] MLM
46] c] departmental store
47] a] shopping malls
48] b] franchisee store
49] c] catalogue marketing
50] d) Telemarketing
51] a] WEB marketing
52] a] Psychological pricing
53] a] psychological appeal
54] c] humor appeal
55] b] gift
56] c) price off
57] d) special offer